Instrument

	Quality	Participants		
1.	Mostly unsecured obligations of banks	Banks	Yield basis. Actual days on a 360-day year.	None.
2.	Promissory notes of firms whose bond rating is usually S&P's AA or the equivalent	Industrial and financial firms	Discount basis. Actual days on 360-day year.	Coupon equivalent (or equivalent bond) yield: 1. *365 day basis:* 365 × d/(360 - (d × T/100)) 2. *360 day basis* 360 × d/(360 - (d × T/100)) *when* d = discount, T = days to maturity
3.	Primary obligation of the accepting bank and a contingent obligation of the drawer and of an endorser	Industrial and financial firms	Discount basis. Actual days on a 360-day year.	Same as for CP.
4.	Certificates of time deposit of commercial banks. Deposits up to $100,000 are insured by FDIC	Banks	Yield basis. Actual days on a 360-day year. Long-term CDs pay interest semi-annually.	None.
5.	Obligaion of international banks	Banks	Yield basis. Actual days on a 360-day year.	None.
6.	U.S. Government obligation	U.S. Government	Discount basis. Actual days on a 360-day year.	Same as for CP.
7.	U.S. Government obligation	U.S. Government	Yield basis. Semi-annual interest payment on a 365-day year basis.	None.
8.	U.S. Government obligation	U.S. Government	Yield basis. Semi-annual interest payment on a 365-day year basis.	None.

EIGHTH EDITION

Interest Rate Spreads & Market Analysis

Tools for Managing and Reducing Rate Exposure in Global Markets

Citicorp
1996

Professional Publishing®

Chicago • London • Singapore

We especially acknowledge Joanne Aron for her vital role in the production of this volume. We would also like to thank Bobby Afkhami, Sandy Batten, Suzanne Crymes, Sougata Datta, Lee Grant, Gokul Hemmady, Steve Karasick, Joan Land, Stephen Leach, Patrick Lin, Neil MacKinnon, Joseph McHugh, David Mooney, Paula Neal, Stuart Rapoport, Jim Rees, Rich Russell, Shubh Saumya, Barry Seeman, Gloria Schneider, and Pat Wiggins. We are also grateful to FAME Information Services, Inc., for its role in the production of this publication.

© 1996 by Citibank, N.A., a subsidiary of Citicorp
Citicorp is a registered trademark.
All rights reserved.
Printed in the United States of America.

The data used in this book, except where otherwise indicated, is provided by FAME Information Services, Inc., 1740 Broadway, 23rd Floor, New York, NY 10019.

The Kenny Index is produced by Kenny Information Systems, Inc., 65 Broadway, New York, NY 10006. The Kenny Index is a registered trademark of Kenny Information Systems, Inc. The data comprising the Kenny Index is copyrighted by Kenny Information Systems, Inc.

The information contained herein was obtained by Citibank, N.A. from independent sources. While precautions were taken in the preparation of this book, no assurance can be given by Citibank, N.A. as to the accuracy or completeness of such information. It is expected that any user of the data contained herein will conduct their own verification of such data and other appropriate due diligence.

ISBN 0-7863-0970-9

Printed in the United States of America
1 2 3 4 5 6 7 8 9 0 BS 3 2 1 0 9 8 7 6

Contents

Preface		vii
Method of Computation		x
Part 1: Spreads Analysis		
I. Absolute Rate Levels		1
	Federal Funds	3
	1 Month LIBOR	4
	1 Month CP Yield	5
	1 Month CD	6
	3 Month LIBOR	7
	3 Month CP Yield	8
	3 Month CD	9
	3 Month BA Yield	10
	3 Month T-Bill Yield	11
	6 Month LIBOR	12
	6 Month CD	13
	6 Month BA Yield	14
	6 Month T-Bill Yield	15
	1 Year LIBOR	16
	1 Year T-Bill Yield	17
	2 Year T-Note	18
	3 Year T-Note	19
	5 Year T-Note	20
	10 Year T-Note	21
	30 Year T-Bond	22
	2 Year Swap Spread	23
	3 Year Swap Spread	24
	5 Year Swap Spread	25
	7 Year Swap Spread	26
	10 Year Swap Spread	27
	Prime	28
	11th District C.O.F. Index	29
	Kenny Index	30
	30 Year GNMA	31
II. Money Market Based Spreads		33
	1 Month LIBOR - Federal Funds	35
	1 Month LIBOR - 1 Month CP Yield	36
	3 Month LIBOR - Federal Funds	37
	3 Month LIBOR - 1 Month LIBOR	38
	3 Month LIBOR - 1 Month CP Yield	39
	3 Month LIBOR - 1 Month CD	40
	3 Month LIBOR - 3 Month CP Yield	41
	3 Month LIBOR - 3 Month CD	42
	3 Month LIBOR - 3 Month BA Yield	43
	Kenny Index As A Percentage of 3 Month LIBOR	44
	3 Month LIBOR - 3 Month T-Bill Yield	45
	3 Month LIBOR - Kenny Index	46
	6 Month LIBOR - 3 Month LIBOR	47
	1 Year LIBOR - 3 Month LIBOR	48
	1 Month CP Yield - Federal Funds	49
	1 Month CD - Federal Funds	50
	1 Month CD - 1 Month CP Yield	51
	3 Month BA Yield - Federal Funds	52
	3 Month BA Yield - 1 Month CP Yield	53

iii

III.	**Treasury Based Spreads**	**55**
	2 Year T-Note - Federal Funds	57
	5 Year T-Note - Federal Funds	58
	5 Year T-Note - 3 Month T-Bill Yield	59
	5 Year T-Note - 6 Month LIBOR	60
	5 Year T-Note - 1 Year T-Bill Yield	61
	10 Year T-Note - 3 Month T-Bill Yield	62
	10 Year T-Note - 6 Month LIBOR	63
	10 Year T-Note - 1 Year T-Bill Yield	64
	10 Year T-Note - 2 Year T-Note	65
	10 Year T-Note - 5 Year T-Note	66
	30 Year T-Bond - 3 Month T-Bill Yield	67
	30 Year T-Bond - 6 Month LIBOR	68
	30 Year T-Bond - 1 Year T-Bill Yield	69
	30 Year T-Bond - 2 Year T-Note	70
	30 Year T-Bond - 10 Year T-Note	71
IV.	**Other Spreads**	**73**
	Prime - Federal Funds	75
	Prime - 1 Month CP Yield	76
	Prime - 3 Month LIBOR	77
	11th District C.O.F. - 1 Month CP Yield	78
	11th District C.O.F. - 3 Month LIBOR	79
	30 Year GNMA - 10 Year T-Note	80
V.	**Corporate Bond Spreads**	**81**
	Industrials	
	AAA-Aaa	83
	AA-Aa	84
	A	85
	BBB-Baa	86
	Utilities	
	AA-Aa	87
	A	88
	BBB-Baa	89
VI.	**Economic Indicators**	**91**
	Chain-weighted Real GDP	93
	Nominal GDP	94
	National Purchasing Managers' Index	95
	Employment (Total Non-farm Payrolls)	96
	Retail Sales	97
	Producer Price Index	98
	Consumer Price Index	99
	Industrial Production	100
	Capacity Utilization	101
	Goods and Services Trade Balance	102
	Housing Starts: Total New Private Housing	103
	Durable Goods Orders	104
	Personal Income	105
	Personal Consumpton Expenditure	106
	Leading Indicators	107
	Money Supply: M1	108
	Money Supply: M2	109

Part 2: Foreign Interest Rates

I. Germany 111
  3 Month LIBOR 113
  6 Month LIBOR 114
  Long Bond Rate 115
  Long Bond Rate - 3 Month LIBOR 116

II. United Kingdom 117
  3 Month LIBOR 119
  6 Month LIBOR 120
  Long Bond Rate 121
  Long Bond Rate - 3 Month LIBOR 122

III. Japan 123
  3 Month LIBOR 125
  6 Month LIBOR 126
  Long Bond Rate 127
  Long Bond Rate - 3 Month LIBOR 128

IV. Switzerland 129
  3 Month LIBOR 131
  6 Month LIBOR 132
  Long Bond Rate 133
  Long Bond Rate - 3 Month LIBOR 134

V. France 135
  3 Month LIBOR 137
  6 Month LIBOR 138
  Long Bond Rate 139
  Long Bond Rate - 3 Month LIBOR 140

VI. Italy 141
  3 Month LIBOR 143
  6 Month LIBOR 144
  Long Bond Rate 145
  Long Bond Rate - 3 Month LIBOR 146

VII. Canada 147
  3 Month LIBOR 149
  6 Month LIBOR 150
  Long Bond Rate 151
  Long Bond Rate - 3 Month LIBOR 152

Part 3: Foreign Exchange Rates
  I. Spot Rates versus Purchasing Power Parity   153
      Germany 155
      United Kingdom 156
      Japan 157
      Switzerland 158
      France 159
      Italy 160
      Canada 161
      Australia 162
      Spain 163

  II. Crosses   165
      GBP/DEM 167
      DEM/JPY 168
      DEM/CHF 169
      DEM/FFR 170
      DEM/ITL 171
      DEM/ESP 172

  III. Exotics   173
      Argentina 175
      Brazil 176
      Chile 177
      Mexico 178
      Venezuela 179
      Korea 180
      Malaysia 181
      Singapore 182
      Indonesia 183
      Thailand 184

Part 4: Equity Markets   185
      Dow Jones Industrial Average 187
      S&P 500 Index 188
      Financial Times Stock Exchange 100 Index 189
      Toronto Stock Exchange 190
      DAX Index 191
      CAC 40 Index 192
      IBEX Index 193
      MIB Index 194
      Nikkei Stock Average 195
      Hang Seng Index 196

Part 5: Commodities   197
      Crude Oil 199
      Natural Gasoline 200
      Aluminum 201
      Copper 202
      Gold 203
      Silver 204

Preface

While there may never be a formula to predict the future movements of market rates, financial managers must still contend daily with the pressures of financing and investing amidst global rate uncertainty. Numerous risk management tools have been developed in the past decade to help financial managers contend with rate volatility, but the proper application of these tools requires an understanding of how rates respond to different economic environments.

Interest Rate Spreads & Market Analysis provides vital data and analysis to foster that understanding by detailing the relative historical performance of key financial indices both in the U.S. and abroad. This work is an analytical tool. Its purpose is not to predict the future course of rates. Rather, *Interest Rate Spreads & Market Analysis* is a resource that can help a manager determine which instruments will perform more favorably under certain interest rate scenarios.

Using the Book

Interest Rate Spreads & Market Analysis provides ten years of historical data for different long- and short-term indices, offering the reader insights into an instrument's behavior through several economic cycles. It includes all of the major U.S. taxable interest rate instruments; the Kenny index for tax exempt bonds; and the 11th District cost of funds, an indicator widely used by the thrift industry.

Interest Rate Spreads & Market Analysis separates analysis of the U.S. interest rates into different sections to provide easy reference. It defines each instrument and provides absolute rate levels over the past decade. The book then compares and contrasts the performance of various instruments, by graphing and discussing key points about the historical relationship of two given instruments. Relationships shown are:

Between Instruments

Two different instruments with the same maturity are compared. The following graph shows 3-month LIBOR versus 3-month commercial paper yields (CP). The spread between these two instruments has been obtained by subtracting the yield on CP from LIBOR. Data back to 1986 indicates that while LIBOR has generally exceeded CP over the past decade, the gap between the yield on the two instruments has narrowed significantly.

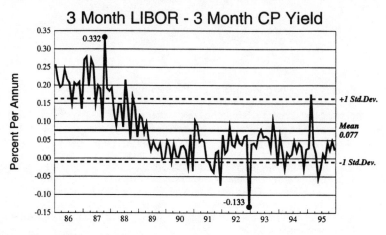

Between Maturities

This section shows two different maturities for the same instrument. The following graph shows 10-year Treasury Note yields versus 2-year Treasury Note yields over the past 10 years. An inverted yield curve is indicated by periods in which the product of this relationship is negative (i.e., the 2-year rate was higher than the 10-year rate).

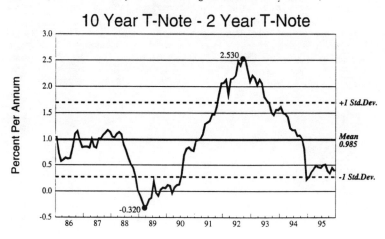

Across Instruments and Maturities

The following graph shows the 5-year Treasury Note yield minus 6-month LIBOR over the past decade. During periods in which the result is negative, LIBOR exceeded 5-year Treasury yields.

Financial managers, analysts, investors, borrowers and students can benefit from the data in *Interest Rate Spreads & Market Analysis*. However, the book is designed primarily as a resource for the financial decision maker.

The book's rate definitions introduce various instruments to those who are unfamiliar with today's wide range of financial tools. The comparisons assist those lenders, borrowers and investors who are evaluating the relative behavior of multiple instruments. For those companies that borrow against one instrument and lend or invest against another, the comparisons are particularly valuable.

Borrowers in both the public and private markets and those whose cash flows can be seriously affected by changes in interest rates should use *Interest Rate Spreads & Market Analysis* as a guide in timing market decisions and weighing funding alternatives.

For the financial manager, the impact of interest rate volatility becomes clearer when the performance of key instruments is viewed over time. *Interest Rate Spreads & Market Analysis* is designed to help demonstrate and explain these relationships — so that they may be used in making future investment, borrowing and portfolio management decisions.

Interest Rate Spreads & Market Analysis has been expanded to include widely quoted foreign interest rates, currency exchange rates, global equity market indices and commodity prices. These changes reflect the increasing globalization of capital markets and the expanded roles played by today's financial manager. This data and accompanying discussions should prove valuable to financial managers who contend with the challenges presented by today's multinational business environment and interlinked economies.

Dipak K. Rastogi
Managing Director
Global Derivatives
Citicorp Securities, Inc.

Method of Computation

At the outset, it should be noted that the basic data used in this book are all monthly averages, not daily rates. While the arithmetic mean of the variables will be the same whether one considers the monthly averages or daily rates, the minimum, maximum and the standard deviation of the series will indeed differ between a daily series and a monthly series. The degree of volatility of the daily average series is likely to be somewhat higher than the monthly average series.

This year, we have adopted a new method of comparing spreads which have different day count bases. In the Absolute Rate Levels section, no day count conversions have been made. In the Money Market Based Spreads section, with the exception of rates which are quoted as discount yields[1], all spreads are computed by using the interest rates as they appear in the market, with no adjustments made to equalize day count bases. Series which are quoted on a discounted basis in the Money Market Based Spreads section have been converted to a money market yield basis using the following formula:

$$\text{Money Market Rate} = \frac{i}{\left(1 - \frac{i}{frequency}\right)}$$

where i = discount rate

For example, a 5% monthly discount rate equals a 5.0209% monthly money market rate.

[1] Bankers' Acceptances, Commercial Paper, and 3, 6, and 12 month Treasury bills are all quoted on a discount yield basis.

PART 1
Spreads Analysis

SECTION I
Absolute Rate Levels

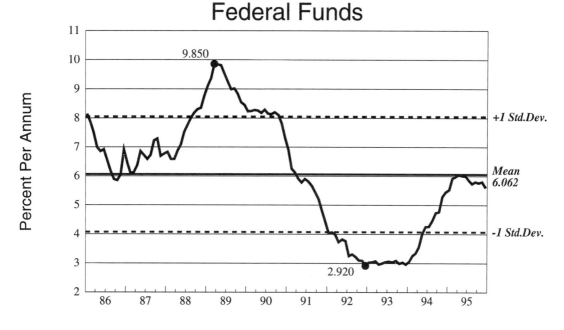

Date Range	Mean	Min.	Max.	Std.Dev.
1986-1995	6.062	2.920	9.850	1.989
1986	6.805	5.850	8.140	0.751
1987	6.658	6.100	7.290	0.370
1988	7.568	6.580	8.760	0.763
1989	9.217	8.450	9.850	0.480
1990	8.099	7.310	8.290	0.279
1991	5.688	4.430	6.910	0.657
1992	3.522	2.920	4.060	0.414
1993	3.023	2.960	3.090	0.040
1994	4.202	3.050	5.450	0.788
1995	5.837	5.530	6.050	0.165

All depository institutions are required to maintain a specified proportion of their liabilities in interest-free reserve balances at the Federal Reserve Bank. Banks with excess reserves lend their surplus to those in need of such reserves via the Federal Funds market. Federal Funds are the most liquid of money market instruments. Interest on Federal Funds accrues on an actual/360 day count basis. The Funds rate is a key policy instrument, and its level at any time reflects the intentions of the Federal Reserve. All other money market rates generally follow the Funds rate. If money growth is to be restrained (accelerated) the Federal Reserve sells (buys) securities, and drains (adds) reserves from (to) the banking system until the funds rate rises (or falls) to the target level. Since October 1979, when the Federal Reserve shifted its attention from monitoring the Fed Funds rate level to managing the growth of monetary aggregates, Fed Funds rate volatility has increased substantially. During 1994, the Federal Funds target was increased 225 basis points in a series of six tightening moves by the Federal Reserve. In 1995, the Fed increased its target by a further 50 basis points, and subsequently eased by the same amount.

1 Month LIBOR

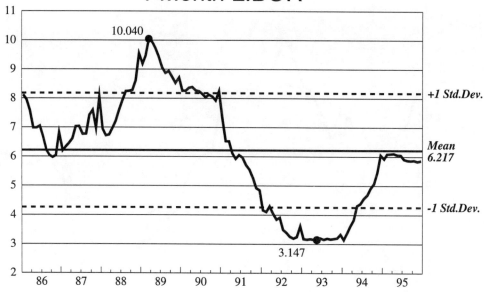

Date Range	Mean	Min.	Max.	Std.Dev.
1986-1995	6.217	3.147	10.040	1.957
1986	6.865	5.969	8.111	0.736
1987	6.935	6.206	8.060	0.542
1988	7.751	6.716	9.536	0.872
1989	9.221	8.533	10.040	0.500
1990	8.193	7.926	8.387	0.136
1991	5.895	4.848	7.326	0.708
1992	3.713	3.193	4.292	0.394
1993	3.189	3.147	3.332	0.049
1994	4.449	3.152	6.048	0.861
1995	5.961	5.831	6.103	0.110

Eurodollars are dollar-denominated deposit liabilities in a bank outside the U.S. or at international banking facilities (IBFs) in the U.S. Foreign banks are active participants in the Eurodollar market. These deposits are subject to neither the reserve requirements nor the FDIC insurance premiums that affect U.S. domestic deposits. Maturities range from money on call to 5 years, but the bulk of the Eurodollar market is comprised of non-negotiable fixed time deposits. Placements typically range from $1 million to $50 million. Changes in short-term U.S. interest rates are almost instantaneously reflected in the Eurodollar rates, which follow the sun from New York to San Francisco, then on to Tokyo, Hong Kong, and Singapore, to Bahrain, on to London, and back again to New York. Eurodollar interest payments are generally calculated using the actual number of days elapsed and a 360-day year. The above series is the average of the London Interbank Offered Rate (LIBOR), recorded at 12:00 noon each day, and published by FAME Information Services, Inc.

1 Month CP Yield

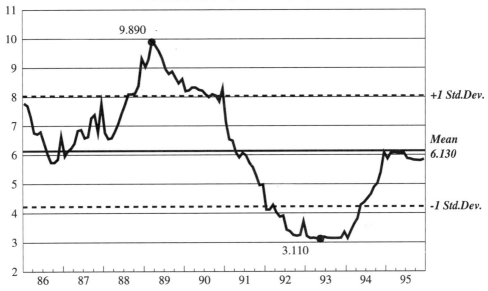

Date Range	Mean	Min.	Max.	Std.Dev.
1986-1995	6.130	3.110	9.890	1.907
1986	6.619	5.740	7.780	0.713
1987	6.728	5.950	7.760	0.538
1988	7.573	6.550	9.310	0.859
1989	9.104	8.470	9.890	0.467
1990	8.153	7.840	8.320	0.146
1991	5.889	4.950	7.120	0.643
1992	3.712	3.220	4.280	0.388
1993	3.167	3.110	3.350	0.063
1994	4.429	3.140	6.080	0.857
1995	5.928	5.800	6.070	0.115

Commercial paper is a short-term unsecured promissory note issued by finance, non-finance, and bank holding companies. Commercial paper is backed by lines of credit from commercial banks. The Securities and Exchange Commission exempts this paper from registration requirements, provided the original maturity is no more than 270 days and the proceeds are used to finance current transactions. The commercial paper market is often the cheapest source of funds for many large corporations. Commercial paper is traded on a discount basis, calculated using actual number of days to maturity and a 360-day year. Yield fluctuations parallel those of the Federal Funds rate, and yield levels are roughly equivalent to CD and Banker's Acceptance rates. The above yields are the average of quotes from six large dealers of commercial paper issued by companies whose bond rating is Standard and Poor's AA or the equivalent, obtained at 11:00 a.m. each day, and published by the Federal Reserve Board in its weekly H.15 bulletin.

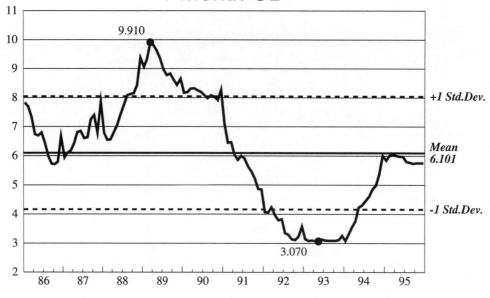

1 Month CD

Date Range	Mean	Min.	Max.	Std.Dev.
1986-1995	6.101	3.070	9.910	1.938
1986	6.615	5.710	7.830	0.733
1987	6.735	5.940	7.860	0.560
1988	7.585	6.550	9.370	0.878
1989	9.112	8.440	9.910	0.487
1990	8.150	7.920	8.320	0.130
1991	5.823	4.840	7.100	0.670
1992	3.636	3.110	4.230	0.402
1993	3.112	3.070	3.260	0.051
1994	4.375	3.080	6.010	0.865
1995	5.866	5.740	6.020	0.120

Efficient cash management by corporations and the concurrent decline of corporate deposits in the banking system led to the development of negotiable certificates of deposit, pioneered by Citibank in August, 1960. CDs are issued in denominations from $100,000 to $1 million, and the typical trading lot is $1 million. CDs have maturities of at least seven days. Interest is calculated using the actual number of days to maturity and a 360-day year. Term CDs pay interest semiannually. Since the elimination of interest rate ceilings on CDs in 1973, CD rates have been determined by market forces. CD rate fluctuations parallel those of the Federal Funds rate. Although generally FDIC-insured, CD yields are usually higher than U.S. Treasury security yields, reflecting the differences in liquidity and credit quality between these instruments. The above series represents secondary market CD rates and is published in the weekly H.15 Federal Reserve bulletin.

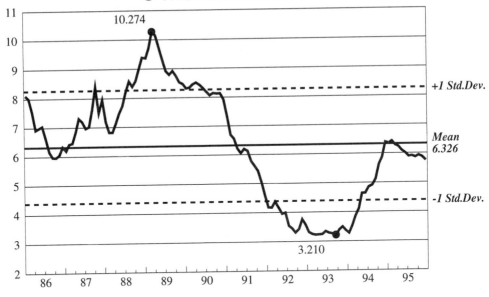

Date Range	Mean	Min.	Max.	Std.Dev.
1986-1995	6.326	3.210	10.274	1.941
1986	6.807	5.962	8.119	0.763
1987	7.150	6.197	8.381	0.645
1988	7.938	6.816	9.381	0.868
1989	9.247	8.466	10.274	0.615
1990	8.245	7.920	8.515	0.177
1991	5.971	4.589	7.332	0.741
1992	3.822	3.304	4.369	0.360
1993	3.300	3.210	3.489	0.083
1994	4.735	3.277	6.384	0.940
1995	6.049	5.744	6.422	0.221

Eurodollars are dollar-denominated deposit liabilities in a bank outside the U.S. or at international banking facilities (IBFs) in the U.S. Foreign banks are active participants in the Eurodollar market. These deposits are subject to neither the reserve requirements nor the FDIC insurance premiums that affect U.S. domestic deposits. Maturities range from money on call to 5 years, but the bulk of the Eurodollar market is comprised of non-negotiable fixed time deposits. Placements typically range from $1 million to $50 million. Changes in short-term U.S. interest rates are almost instantaneously reflected in the Eurodollar rates, which follow the sun from New York to San Francisco, then on to Tokyo, Hong Kong, and Singapore, to Bahrain, on to London, and back again to New York. Eurodollar interest payments are generally calculated using the actual number of days elapsed and a 360 day year. The above series is the average of the London Interbank Offered Rate (LIBOR), recorded at 12:00 noon each day, and published by FAME Information Services, Inc.

SPREADS ANALYSIS

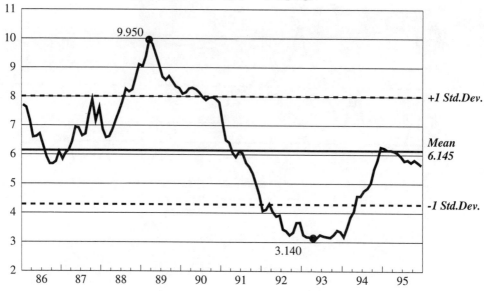

3 Month CP Yield

Date Range	Mean	Min.	Max.	Std.Dev.
1986-1995	6.145	3.140	9.950	1.861
1986	6.495	5.680	7.710	0.721
1987	6.813	5.840	7.890	0.631
1988	7.656	6.580	9.110	0.845
1989	8.989	8.290	9.950	0.560
1990	8.061	7.800	8.300	0.165
1991	5.865	4.610	7.100	0.680
1992	3.753	3.240	4.300	0.350
1993	3.224	3.140	3.400	0.084
1994	4.659	3.190	6.260	0.922
1995	5.933	5.640	6.220	0.199

Commercial paper is a short-term unsecured promissory note issued by finance, non-finance, and bank holding companies. Commercial paper is backed by lines of credit from commercial banks. The Securities and Exchange Commission exempts this paper from registration requirements, provided that the original maturity is no more than 270 days and that the proceeds are used to finance current transactions. The commercial paper market is often the cheapest source of funds for many large corporations. Commercial paper is traded on a discount basis, calculated using actual number of days to maturity and a 360-day year. Yield fluctuations parallel those of the Federal Funds rate, and yield levels are roughly equivalent to CD and Banker's Acceptance rates. The above yields are the average of quotes from six large dealers of commercial paper, issued by companies whose bond rating is Standard and Poor's AA or the equivalent, obtained at 11:00 a.m. each day, and published by the Federal Reserve Board in its weekly H.15 bulletin.

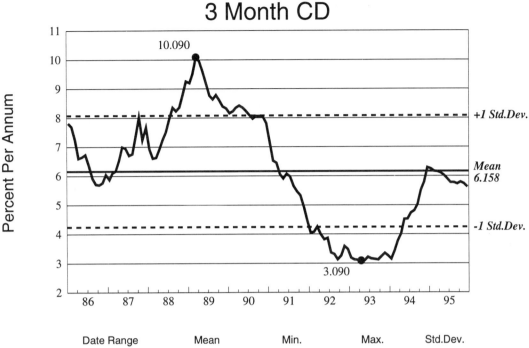

Date Range	Mean	Min.	Max.	Std.Dev.
1986-1995	6.158	3.090	10.090	1.921
1986	6.518	5.690	7.820	0.750
1987	6.861	5.870	8.020	0.647
1988	7.728	6.600	9.250	0.883
1989	9.085	8.320	10.090	0.596
1990	8.148	7.820	8.420	0.175
1991	5.835	4.470	7.170	0.729
1992	3.682	3.130	4.250	0.373
1993	3.174	3.090	3.350	0.079
1994	4.629	3.150	6.290	0.947
1995	5.917	5.620	6.240	0.209

Efficient cash management by corporations and the concurrent decline of corporate deposits in the banking system led to the development of negotiable certificates of deposit (CDs), pioneered by Citibank in August, 1960. CDs are issued in denominations from $100,000 to $1 million, and the typical trading lot is $1 million. CDs have maturities of at least seven days. In December, 1990, reserve requirements on term deposits were eliminated. Interest is calculated using actual number of days to maturity and a 360-day year. Term CDs pay interest semiannually. Since the elimination of interest rate ceilings on CDs in 1973, CD rates have been determined by market forces. CD rate fluctuations parallel those of the Federal Funds rate. Although generally FDIC-insured, CD yields are usually higher than U.S. Treasury security yields, reflecting the differences in the liquidity and credit quality between these instruments. The above series represents secondary market CD rates and is published in the weekly H.15 Federal Reserve bulletin.

3 Month BA Yield

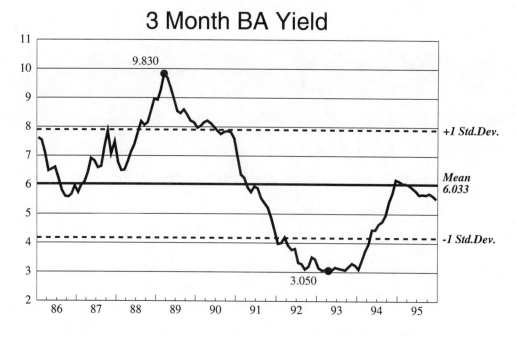

Date Range	Mean	Min.	Max.	Std.Dev.
1986-1995	6.033	3.050	9.830	1.861
1986	6.393	5.580	7.620	0.723
1987	6.743	5.740	7.850	0.631
1988	7.562	6.490	8.960	0.835
1989	8.868	8.150	9.830	0.563
1990	7.933	7.600	8.210	0.179
1991	5.705	4.420	6.960	0.687
1992	3.623	3.100	4.190	0.362
1993	3.128	3.050	3.290	0.077
1994	4.561	3.100	6.180	0.925
1995	5.816	5.520	6.120	0.199

A banker's acceptance (BA) is an irrevocable primary obligation of the accepting bank and a contingent obligation of the drawer and of any endorsers whose names appear on it. Historically, most BAs have arisen in the course of international trade. BA maturities range from 30 to 180 days, with 90 days being most common. BAs are eligible collateral for borrowing from the Federal Reserve Banks. BA rates are quoted on a discount basis, and yields are calculated using actual number of days to maturity and a 360-day year. Besides the discount, BAs involve additional fees payable to the accepting bank. The effective cost of BAs continues to be lower than the effective cost of Prime-based loans, giving rise to the popularity of BAs. BA yield fluctuations track the fluctuations in other money market rates, notably the CD rate. The above series is derived from the weekly H.15 bulletin published by the Federal Reserve Board.

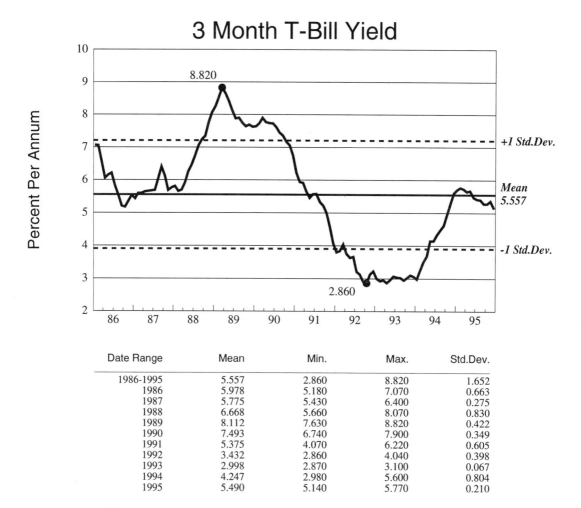

Date Range	Mean	Min.	Max.	Std.Dev.
1986-1995	5.557	2.860	8.820	1.652
1986	5.978	5.180	7.070	0.663
1987	5.775	5.430	6.400	0.275
1988	6.668	5.660	8.070	0.830
1989	8.112	7.630	8.820	0.422
1990	7.493	6.740	7.900	0.349
1991	5.375	4.070	6.220	0.605
1992	3.432	2.860	4.040	0.398
1993	2.998	2.870	3.100	0.067
1994	4.247	2.980	5.600	0.804
1995	5.490	5.140	5.770	0.210

Treasury bills are U.S. Government obligations sold in minimum initial denominations of $10,000, followed by $1,000 increments. They are sold on a discount basis, calculated using actual number of days to maturity and a 360-day year. Treasury bills are risk-free instruments with an active secondary market. Treasury bill interest is exempt from state and local taxes. The Treasury bill yield is largely determined by supply and demand conditions and by market expectations regarding scheduled offerings to refinance maturing issues or to finance current Federal deficits. Historically, the yield fluctuations have correlated closely with changes in the Federal Funds rate. Significant shifts in the Federal Reserve's monetary policy have a strong impact on the Treasury bill rate. The above yields are the average of the closing bid rates quoted by five of the primary dealers in U.S. government securities, published weekly in the H.15 bulletin of the Federal Reserve Board.

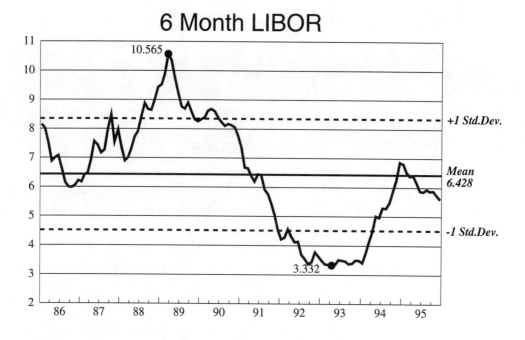

6 Month LIBOR

Date Range	Mean	Min.	Max.	Std.Dev.
1986-1995	6.428	3.332	10.565	1.918
1986	6.807	5.983	8.153	0.774
1987	7.284	6.169	8.482	0.700
1988	8.105	6.894	9.432	0.846
1989	9.240	8.262	10.565	0.772
1990	8.286	7.747	8.679	0.272
1991	6.069	4.542	7.345	0.772
1992	3.920	3.372	4.554	0.390
1993	3.426	3.332	3.509	0.071
1994	5.064	3.411	6.864	1.015
1995	6.084	5.588	6.795	0.365

Eurodollars are dollar-denominated deposit liabilities in a bank outside the U.S. or at international banking facilities (IBFs) in the U.S. Foreign banks are active participants in the Eurodollar market. These deposits are subject to neither the reserve requirements nor the FDIC insurance premiums that affect U.S. domestic deposits. Maturities range from money on call to 5 years, but the bulk of the Eurodollar market is comprised of non-negotiable fixed time deposits. Placements typically range from $1 million to $50 million. Changes in short-term U.S. interest rates are almost instantaneously reflected in the Eurodollar rates, which follow the sun from New York to San Francisco, then on to Tokyo, Hong Kong, and Singapore, to Bahrain, on to London, and back again to New York. Eurodollar interest payments are generally calculated using the actual number of days elapsed and a 360-day year. The above series is the average of the London Interbank Offered Rate (LIBOR), recorded at 12:00 noon each day, and published by FAME Information Services, Inc.

6 Month CD

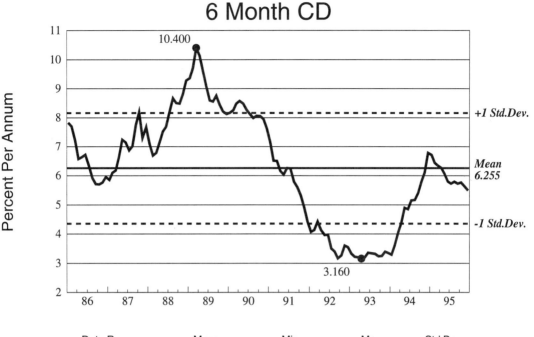

Date Range	Mean	Min.	Max.	Std.Dev.
1986-1995	6.255	3.160	10.400	1.904
1986	6.508	5.700	7.830	0.756
1987	6.998	5.850	8.190	0.709
1988	7.903	6.690	9.280	0.864
1989	9.081	8.120	10.400	0.756
1990	8.171	7.640	8.570	0.263
1991	5.910	4.410	7.170	0.757
1992	3.764	3.170	4.420	0.398
1993	3.280	3.160	3.390	0.077
1994	4.956	3.290	6.780	1.018
1995	5.981	5.490	6.710	0.377

Efficient cash management by corporations and the concurrent decline of corporate deposits in the banking system led to the development of negotiable certificates of deposit (CDs), pioneered by Citibank in August, 1960. CDs are issued in denominations from $100,000 to $1 million, and the normal trading lot is $1 million. CDs have maturities of at least seven days. In December, 1990, reserve requirements on term deposits were eliminated. Interest is calculated using the actual number of days to maturity and a 360-day year. Term CDs pay interest semiannually. Since the elimination of interest rate ceilings on CDs in 1973, CD rates have been determined by market forces. CD rate fluctuations parallel those of the Federal Funds rate. Although generally FDIC-insured, CD yields are generally higher than U.S. Treasury security yields, reflecting the differences in liquidity and credit quality of these instruments. The above series represents secondary market CD rates and is published in the weekly H.15 Federal Reserve bulletin.

SPREADS ANALYSIS

Date Range	Mean	Min.	Max.	Std.Dev.
1986-1995	6.029	3.100	9.870	1.791
1986	6.292	5.520	7.550	0.712
1987	6.772	5.650	7.920	0.678
1988	7.593	6.490	8.830	0.799
1989	8.666	7.780	9.870	0.696
1990	7.798	7.250	8.180	0.261
1991	5.674	4.280	6.840	0.697
1992	3.672	3.130	4.290	0.372
1993	3.208	3.100	3.320	0.072
1994	4.819	3.210	6.530	0.965
1995	5.800	5.340	6.450	0.345

A banker's acceptance (BA) is an irrevocable primary obligation of the accepting bank and a contingent obligation of the drawer and of any endorsers whose names appear on it. Historically, most BAs have arisen in the course of international trade. BA maturities range from 30 to 180 days, with 90 days being most common. BAs are eligible collateral for borrowing from the Federal Reserve Banks. BA rates are quoted on a discount basis, and yields are calculated using actual number of days to maturity and a 360-day year. Besides the discount, BAs involve additional fees payable to the accepting bank. The effective cost of BAs continues to be lower than the effective cost of Prime-based loans, giving rise to the popularity of BAs. BA yield fluctuations track the fluctuations in other money market rates, notably the CD rate. The above series is derived from the weekly H.15 bulletin published by the Federal Reserve Board.

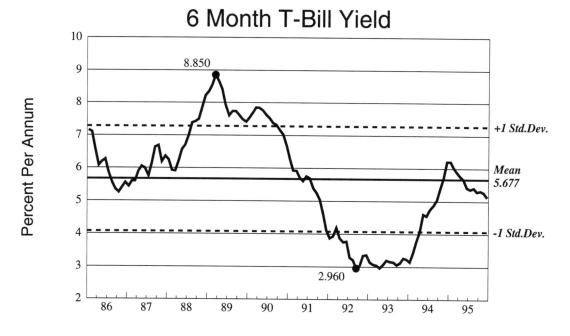

Date Range	Mean	Min.	Max.	Std.Dev.
1986-1995	5.677	2.960	8.850	1.603
1986	6.030	5.260	7.160	0.657
1987	6.030	5.440	6.690	0.402
1988	6.913	5.910	8.220	0.770
1989	8.031	7.420	8.850	0.502
1990	7.453	6.700	7.850	0.352
1991	5.441	4.100	6.280	0.612
1992	3.547	2.960	4.180	0.394
1993	3.123	2.970	3.260	0.083
1994	4.633	3.150	6.210	0.912
1995	5.566	5.130	6.210	0.341

Treasury bills are U.S. Government obligations sold in minimum initial denominations of $10,000, followed by $1,000 increments. They are risk-free instruments with an active secondary market. Treasury bill interest is exempt from state and local taxes. The Treasury bill yield is largely determined by supply and demand conditions and by market expectations regarding scheduled offerings to refinance maturing issues or to finance current Federal deficits. Historically, the yield fluctuations have correlated closely with changes in the Federal Funds rate. Significant shifts in the Federal Reserve's monetary policy have a strong impact on the Treasury bill rate. The above yields are the average of the closing bid rates quoted by five of the primary dealers in U.S. government securities, published weekly in the H.15 bulletin of the Federal Reserve Board.

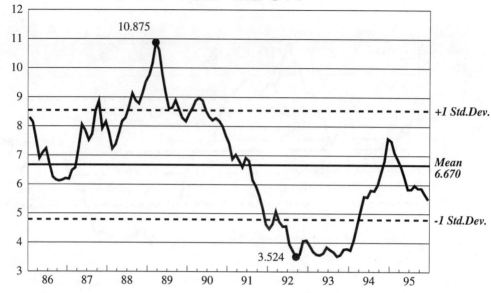

1 Year LIBOR

Date Range	Mean	Min.	Max.	Std.Dev.
1986-1995	6.670	3.524	10.875	1.877
1986	6.905	6.125	8.293	0.779
1987	7.594	6.184	8.866	0.830
1988	8.388	7.234	9.518	0.739
1989	9.293	8.166	10.875	0.919
1990	8.416	7.676	8.973	0.387
1991	6.332	4.631	7.413	0.840
1992	4.245	3.524	5.065	0.493
1993	3.694	3.531	3.893	0.117
1994	5.587	3.747	7.580	1.100
1995	6.242	5.481	7.494	0.635

Eurodollars are dollar-denominated deposits in a bank outside the United States or at International Banking Facilities (IBFs) in the U.S. Foreign banks are active participants in the Eurodollar market. These deposits are subject to neither the reserve requirements nor the FDIC insurance premiums that affect U.S. domestic deposits. Maturities range from money on call to 5 years, but the bulk of the Eurodollar market is comprised of non-negotiable fixed time deposits. Placements typically range from $1 million to $50 million. Changes in short-term U.S. interest rates are instantaneously reflected in the Eurodollar rates. Eurodollar interest payments are generally calculated using actual number of days elapsed and a 360-day year. The above series is the average of the London Interbank Offered Rate (LIBOR), recorded at 12:00 each day, and published by FAME Information Services, Inc.

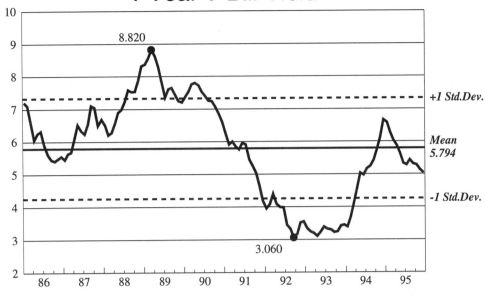

Date Range	Mean	Min.	Max.	Std.Dev.
1986-1995	5.794	3.060	8.820	1.538
1986	6.078	5.410	7.210	0.635
1987	6.322	5.460	7.110	0.531
1988	7.128	6.210	8.320	0.664
1989	7.922	7.210	8.820	0.583
1990	7.348	6.610	7.800	0.368
1991	5.517	4.170	6.250	0.627
1992	3.714	3.060	4.400	0.421
1993	3.292	3.110	3.450	0.100
1994	5.014	3.390	6.670	0.962
1995	5.603	5.030	6.590	0.489

Treasury bills are U.S. Government obligations sold in minimum initial denominations of $10,000, followed by $1,000 increments. They are sold on a discount basis, calculated using actual number of days to maturity and a 360-day year. Treasury bills are risk-free instruments with an active secondary market. Treasury bill interest is exempt from state and local taxes. The Treasury bill yield is determined by supply and demand conditions and market expectations of scheduled offerings to refinance maturing issues or to finance current Federal deficits. The yield on Treasury instruments is closely correlated with changes in the Federal Funds rate. As a result, significant shifts in the Federal Reserve's monetary policy have a strong impact on the Treasury bill rate. The above yields are the average of the closing bid rates quoted by five of the primary dealers in U.S. government securities, published weekly in the H.15 bulletin of the Federal Reserve Board.

SPREADS ANALYSIS

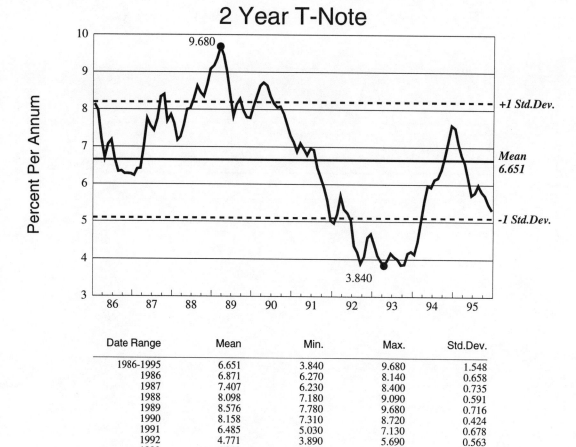

Date Range	Mean	Min.	Max.	Std.Dev.
1986-1995	6.651	3.840	9.680	1.548
1986	6.871	6.270	8.140	0.658
1987	7.407	6.230	8.400	0.735
1988	8.098	7.180	9.090	0.591
1989	8.576	7.780	9.680	0.716
1990	8.158	7.310	8.720	0.424
1991	6.485	5.030	7.130	0.678
1992	4.771	3.890	5.690	0.563
1993	4.048	3.840	4.390	0.166
1994	5.936	4.140	7.590	1.024
1995	6.161	5.320	7.510	0.684

The U.S. Treasury issues notes with initial maturities ranging from 2 years to 10 years. Treasury Notes pay interest semi-annually on a 365-day year basis. The 2 and 3 year Treasury Notes are U.S. Government obligations sold in minimum initial denominations of $5,000, followed by $1,000 increments. They are primarily held in book entry form at the regional Federal Reserve Banks and can be readily transferred to buyers. Prices are quoted in 32nds. Yields are determined by supply and demand conditions and by interest rate expectations. Treasury securities are risk-free instruments with an active secondary market, and their yields reflect their exemption from state and local income taxes. The above yields are derived from a constant maturity yield curve, based upon closing bid prices quoted by at least five dealers. The yields are published by the Federal Reserve Board in its weekly H.15 bulletin.

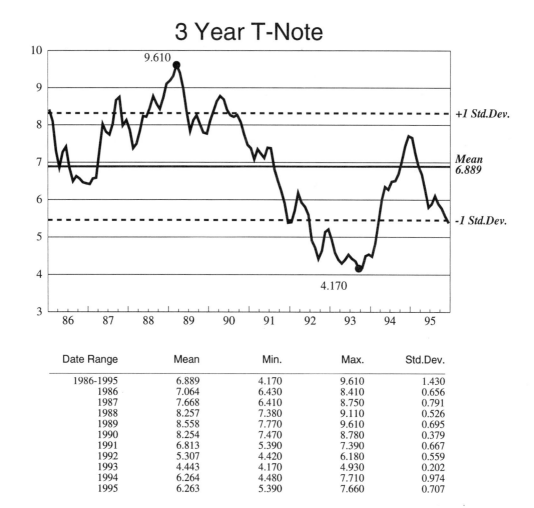

Date Range	Mean	Min.	Max.	Std.Dev.
1986-1995	6.889	4.170	9.610	1.430
1986	7.064	6.430	8.410	0.656
1987	7.668	6.410	8.750	0.791
1988	8.257	7.380	9.110	0.526
1989	8.558	7.770	9.610	0.695
1990	8.254	7.470	8.780	0.379
1991	6.813	5.390	7.390	0.667
1992	5.307	4.420	6.180	0.559
1993	4.443	4.170	4.930	0.202
1994	6.264	4.480	7.710	0.974
1995	6.263	5.390	7.660	0.707

The U.S. Treasury issues notes with initial maturities ranging from 2 years to 10 years Treasury Notes pay interest semi-annually on a 365-day year basis. The 2 and 3 year Treasury Notes are U.S. Government obligations sold in minimum initial denominations of $5,000, followed by $1,000 increments. They are primarily held in book entry form at the regional Federal Reserve Banks and can be readily transferred to buyers. Prices are quoted in 32nds. Yields are determined by supply and demand conditions and by interest rate expectations. Treasury securities are risk-free instruments with an active secondary market, and their yields reflect their exemption from state and local income taxes. The above yields are derived from a constant maturity yield curve, based upon closing bid prices quoted by at least five dealers. The yields are published by the Federal Reserve Board in its weekly H.15 bulletin.

SPREADS ANALYSIS

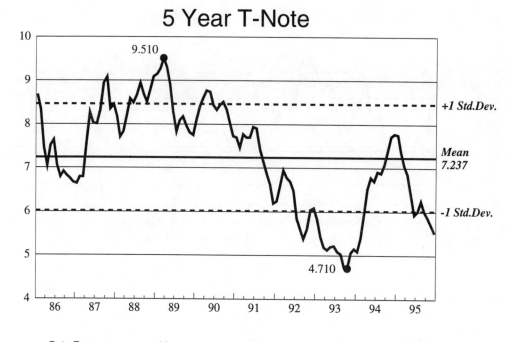

5 Year T-Note

Date Range	Mean	Min.	Max.	Std.Dev.
1986-1995	7.237	4.710	9.510	1.221
1986	7.311	6.670	8.680	0.647
1987	7.935	6.640	9.080	0.823
1988	8.472	7.710	9.090	0.422
1989	8.504	7.750	9.510	0.670
1990	8.370	7.730	8.770	0.298
1991	7.370	6.190	7.940	0.554
1992	6.188	5.380	6.950	0.516
1993	5.148	4.710	5.830	0.293
1994	6.683	5.090	7.780	0.843
1995	6.391	5.510	7.760	0.712

The U.S. Treasury issues notes with initial maturities ranging from 2 years to 10 years. Treasury Notes pay interest semi-annually on a 365-day year basis. The 5 through 10 year Treasury Notes are issued in denominations of at least $1,000. Treasury securities are primarily held in book entry form at the regional Federal Reserve Banks and can be readily transferred to buyers. Prices are quoted in 32nds. Yields are determined by supply and demand conditions and by interest rate expectations. Treasury securities are risk-free instruments with an active secondary market, and their yields reflect their exemption from state and local income taxes. The above yields are derived from a constant maturity yield curve, based upon closing bid prices quoted by at least five dealers. The yields are published by the Federal Reserve Board in its weekly H.15 bulletin.

SPREADS ANALYSIS

10 Year T-Note

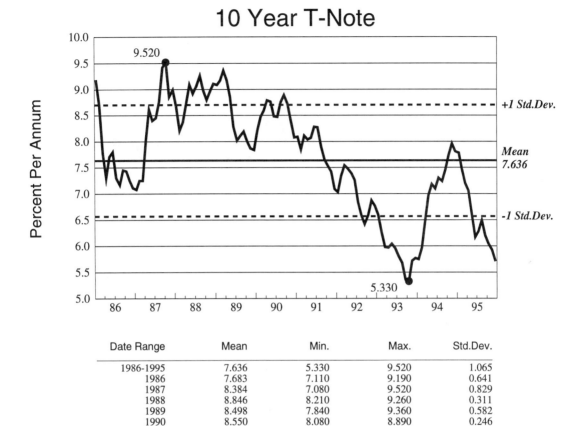

Date Range	Mean	Min.	Max.	Std.Dev.
1986-1995	7.636	5.330	9.520	1.065
1986	7.683	7.110	9.190	0.641
1987	8.384	7.080	9.520	0.829
1988	8.846	8.210	9.260	0.311
1989	8.498	7.840	9.360	0.582
1990	8.550	8.080	8.890	0.246
1991	7.858	7.090	8.280	0.367
1992	7.010	6.420	7.540	0.384
1993	5.873	5.330	6.600	0.353
1994	7.080	5.750	7.960	0.697
1995	6.580	5.710	7.780	0.656

The U.S. Treasury issues notes with initial maturities ranging from 2 years to 10 years. Treasury Notes pay interest semi-annually on a 365-day year basis. The 5 through 10 year Treasury Notes are issued in denominations of at least $1,000. Treasury securities are primarily held in book entry form at the regional Federal Reserve Banks and can be readily transferred to buyers. Prices are quoted in 32nds. Yields are determined by supply and demand conditions and by interest rate expectations. Treasury securities are risk free instruments with an active secondary market, and their yields reflect their exemption from state and local income taxes. The above yields are derived from a constant maturity yield curve, based upon closing bid prices quoted by at least five dealers. The yields are published by the Federal Reserve Board in its weekly H.15 bulletin.

SPREADS ANALYSIS

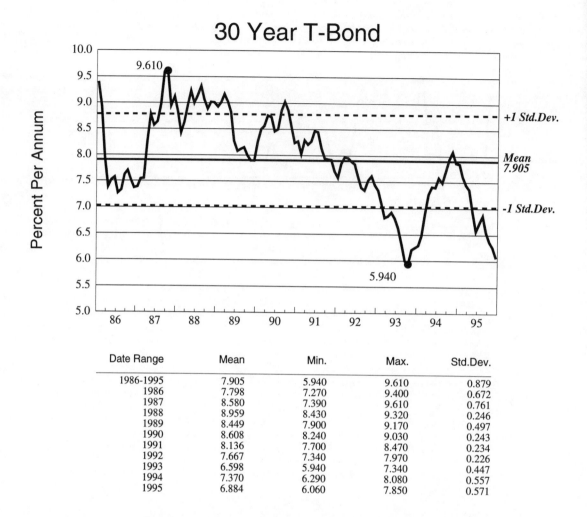

Date Range	Mean	Min.	Max.	Std.Dev.
1986-1995	7.905	5.940	9.610	0.879
1986	7.798	7.270	9.400	0.672
1987	8.580	7.390	9.610	0.761
1988	8.959	8.430	9.320	0.246
1989	8.449	7.900	9.170	0.497
1990	8.608	8.240	9.030	0.243
1991	8.136	7.700	8.470	0.234
1992	7.667	7.340	7.970	0.226
1993	6.598	5.940	7.340	0.447
1994	7.370	6.290	8.080	0.557
1995	6.884	6.060	7.850	0.571

Treasury bonds generally have initial maturities exceeding 10 years and pay interest semi-annually on an actual/365-day count basis. The 30 year Treasury Bond is issued in denominations of at least $1,000. Treasury securities are primarily held in book entry form at the regional Federal Reserve Banks and can be readily transferred to buyers. Prices are quoted in 32nds. Yields are determined by supply and demand conditions and by interest rate expectations. Treasury securities are risk-free instruments with an active secondary market, and their yields reflect their exemption from state and local income taxes. The 30 year T-Bond is now auctioned only semi-annually. The above yields are derived from a constant maturity yield curve, based upon closing bid prices quoted by at least five dealers. The yields are published by the Federal Reserve Board in its weekly H.15 bulletin.

2 Year Swap Spread (Offer)

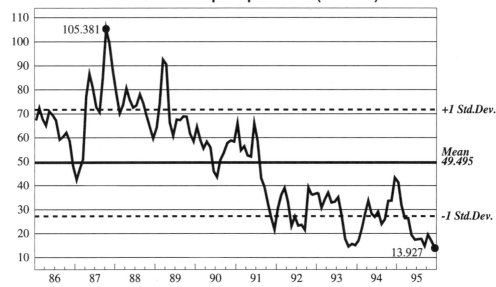

Date Range	Mean	Min.	Max.	Std.Dev.
1986-1995	49.495	13.927	105.381	22.287
1986	64.055	48.333	72.385	6.759
1987	75.461	42.526	105.381	20.010
1988	72.557	59.619	80.600	6.019
1989	70.099	58.390	92.430	10.843
1990	55.147	43.571	64.400	5.897
1991	47.512	21.700	66.000	14.715
1992	30.249	21.591	39.182	6.798
1993	27.540	14.550	37.048	9.107
1994	28.807	17.095	43.227	6.723
1995	21.924	13.927	41.284	8.088

U.S. Dollar Interest Rate Swaps provide for an exchange of interest payments between counterparties for a specified time period. No principal exchange occurs. The swap spreads above assume that semi-annual fixed interest rate payments calculated using a 365-day year are exchanged for 3 month LIBOR-based payments. Swap rates are quoted as a spread, in basis points per annum, over the relevant U.S. Treasury security. Swap spreads are determined by supply and demand conditions in the swap market.

SPREADS ANALYSIS

3 Year Swap Spread (Offer)

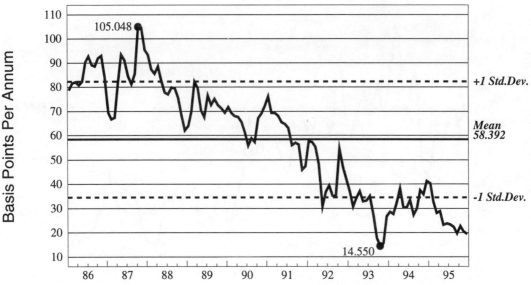

Date Range	Mean	Min.	Max.	Std.Dev.
1986-1995	58.392	14.550	105.048	23.867
1986	86.259	78.750	92.889	5.160
1987	85.461	66.722	105.048	13.164
1988	79.760	62.048	93.211	8.684
1989	72.578	63.950	82.170	5.095
1990	65.295	55.762	72.118	5.616
1991	61.552	46.000	76.050	9.151
1992	45.225	30.810	57.409	10.019
1993	28.507	14.550	37.048	8.239
1994	32.740	27.391	41.364	4.530
1995	25.446	19.503	40.336	6.156

U.S. Dollar Interest Rate Swaps provide for an exchange of interest payments between counterparties for a specified time period. No principal exchange occurs. The swap spreads above assume that semi-annual fixed interest rate payments calculated using a 365-day year are exchanged for 3 month LIBOR-based payments. Swap rates are quoted as a spread, in basis points per annum, over the relevant U.S. Treasury security. Swap spreads are determined by supply and demand conditions in the swap market.

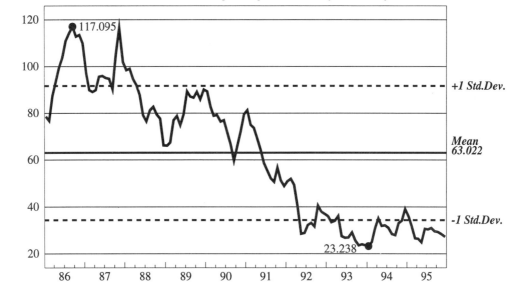

5 Year Swap Spread (Offer)

Date Range	Mean	Min.	Max.	Std.Dev.
1986-1995	63.022	23.238	117.095	28.684
1986	101.454	76.769	117.095	14.347
1987	96.759	89.136	116.450	7.937
1988	84.543	66.238	99.000	9.933
1989	80.974	66.050	90.050	8.405
1990	75.002	59.667	89.350	8.084
1991	61.469	49.000	81.250	10.926
1992	38.692	28.571	52.000	8.753
1993	28.923	23.600	36.095	4.772
1994	31.016	23.238	39.091	4.358
1995	29.357	24.984	35.839	2.905

U.S. Dollar Interest Rate Swaps provide for an exchange of interest payments between counterparties for a specified time period. No principal exchange occurs. The swap spreads above assume that semi-annual fixed interest rate payments calculated using a 365-day year are exchanged for 3 month LIBOR-based payments. Swap rates are quoted as a spread, in basis points per annum, over the relevant U.S. Treasury security.

The pattern of swap spreads in longer maturities (4 - 10 years) reflects supply and demand pressures created by the absolute level of U.S. Treasury rates, the shape of the Treasury yield curve, credit perceptions, rate views, activity in the Eurobond and domestic markets, as well as speculation. For example, the stock market crash in October, 1987, and the subsequent decline in interest rates brought many fixed rate payers to the swap market. This increased demand caused swap spreads to widen by 30 basis points almost overnight. Once the market stabilized, swap spreads began to return to prior levels.

SPREADS ANALYSIS

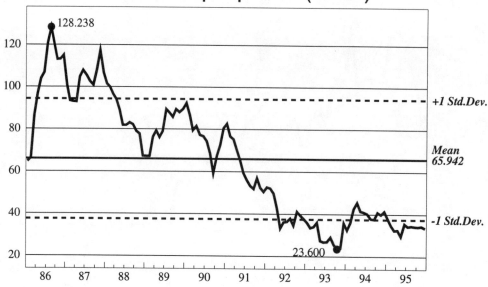

Date Range	Mean	Min.	Max.	Std.Dev.
1986-1995	65.942	23.600	128.238	28.346
1986	102.924	64.563	128.238	20.817
1987	102.784	92.952	117.250	7.214
1988	86.172	67.286	101.526	10.182
1989	81.270	67.190	89.530	8.339
1990	76.405	59.278	92.250	8.864
1991	62.560	50.600	82.550	11.104
1992	41.524	33.286	52.636	7.031
1993	29.938	23.600	36.095	4.843
1994	39.775	32.524	45.429	3.347
1995	34.033	29.774	37.790	1.925

U.S. Dollar Interest Rate Swaps provide for an exchange of interest payments between counterparties for a specified time period. No principal exchange occurs. The swap spreads above assume that semi-annual fixed interest rate payments calculated using a 365-day year are exchanged for 3 month LIBOR-based payments. Swap rates are quoted as a spread, in basis points per annum, over the relevant U.S. Treasury security. The last 7 year Treasury note was issued in April, 1993. Since then, the 7 year swap spread is quoted as a spread to the interpolated 7 year Treasury yield (the point between the 5 year Treasury yield and the 10 year Treasury yield).

The pattern of swap spreads in longer maturities (4 - 10 years) reflects supply and demand pressures created by the absolute level of U.S. Treasury rates, the shape of the Treasury yield curve, credit perceptions, rate views, activity in the Eurobond and domestic markets, as well as speculation. For example, the stock market crash in October, 1987, and the subsequent decline in interest rates brought many fixed rate payers to the swap market. This increased demand caused swap spreads to widen by 30 basis points almost overnight. Once the market stabilized, swap spreads began to return to prior levels.

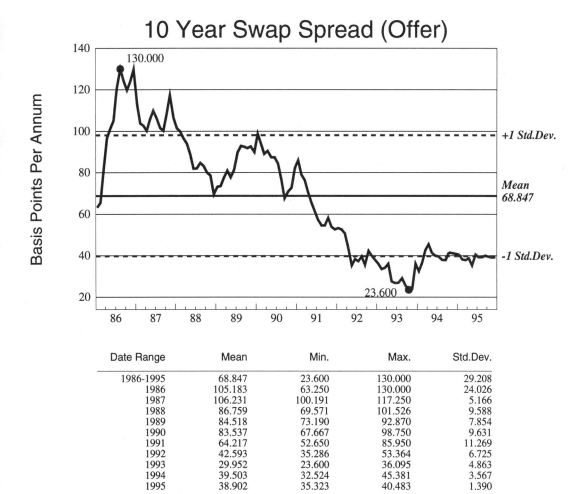

Date Range	Mean	Min.	Max.	Std.Dev.
1986-1995	68.847	23.600	130.000	29.208
1986	105.183	63.250	130.000	24.026
1987	106.231	100.191	117.250	5.166
1988	86.759	69.571	101.526	9.588
1989	84.518	73.190	92.870	7.854
1990	83.537	67.667	98.750	9.631
1991	64.217	52.650	85.950	11.269
1992	42.593	35.286	53.364	6.725
1993	29.952	23.600	36.095	4.863
1994	39.503	32.524	45.381	3.567
1995	38.902	35.323	40.483	1.390

U.S. Dollar Interest Rate Swaps provide for an exchange of interest payments between counterparties for a specified time period. No principal exchange occurs. The swap spreads above assume that semi-annual fixed interest rate payments calculated using a 365-day year are exchanged for 3 month LIBOR-based payments. Swap rates are quoted as a spread, in basis points per annum, over the relevant U.S. Treasury security.

The pattern of swap spreads in longer maturities (4 - 10 years) reflects supply and demand pressures created by the absolute level of U.S. Treasury rates, the shape of the Treasury yield curve, credit perceptions, rate views, activity in the Eurobond and domestic markets, as well as speculation. For example, the stock market crash in October, 1987, and the subsequent decline in interest rates brought many fixed rate payers to the swap market. This increased demand caused swap spreads to widen by 30 basis points almost overnight. Once the market stabilized, swap spreads began to fall back to prior levels.

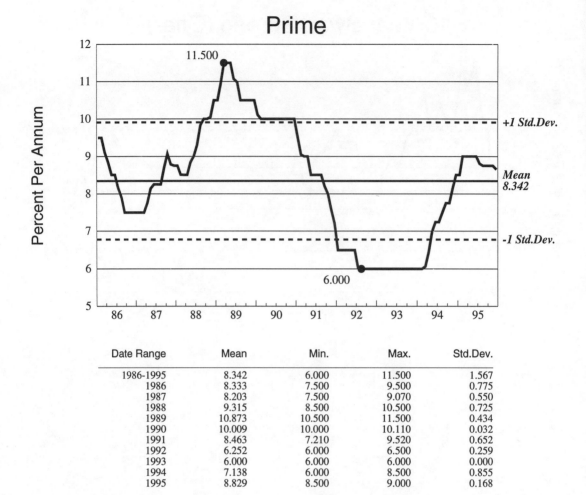

Date Range	Mean	Min.	Max.	Std.Dev.
1986-1995	8.342	6.000	11.500	1.567
1986	8.333	7.500	9.500	0.775
1987	8.203	7.500	9.070	0.550
1988	9.315	8.500	10.500	0.725
1989	10.873	10.500	11.500	0.434
1990	10.009	10.000	10.110	0.032
1991	8.463	7.210	9.520	0.652
1992	6.252	6.000	6.500	0.259
1993	6.000	6.000	6.000	0.000
1994	7.138	6.000	8.500	0.855
1995	8.829	8.500	9.000	0.168

The Prime rate is the base lending rate charged by large banks on commercial loans. Most recently, Prime has also developed as a basis for consumer loans such as credit cards. The rate is a managed rate, rather than a market rate, set by banks. It reflects the cost of funds to commercial banks, including the cost of reserve requirements, FDIC premiums, and bank operations. The Prime rate has generally tended to rise in periods of economic expansion and decline in periods of economic contraction. Prime rate averages are published in the weekly Federal Reserve H.15 bulletin. Interest is settled quarterly, on the basis of actual number of days elapsed in a 360-day year.

SPREADS ANALYSIS

11th Dist. C.O.F. Index

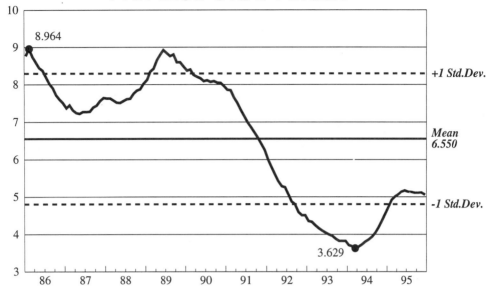

Date Range	Mean	Min.	Max.	Std.Dev.
1986-1995	6.550	3.629	8.964	1.742
1986	8.235	7.509	8.964	0.488
1987	7.373	7.223	7.645	0.132
1988	7.678	7.508	8.020	0.159
1989	8.613	8.130	8.923	0.234
1990	8.152	7.960	8.400	0.135
1991	7.097	6.250	7.860	0.554
1992	5.146	4.508	6.000	0.504
1993	4.047	3.822	4.360	0.197
1994	3.875	3.629	4.367	0.237
1995	5.062	4.747	5.179	0.121

The 11th District Cost of Funds Index is the monthly weighted average cost of funds of the 11th District (Federal Home Loan Banks) savings and loan associations. The index represents the cost of funds to the thrift industry, and it is derived from interest paid on savings accounts, Federal Home Loan Bank advances, and other borrowed money, adjusted for variations in the number of days in each month. The index is published by the Federal Home Loan Bank of San Francisco. The cost of funds for savings and loan associations, as seen above, has generally lagged other money market rates. In the past, this lag has occurred because a major component of the index, interest paid on savings accounts, did not fluctuate as rapidly as other money market interest rates.

SPREADS ANALYSIS

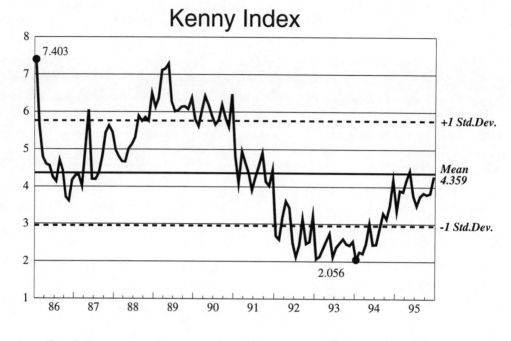

Kenny Index

Date Range	Mean	Min.	Max.	Std.Dev.
1986-1995	4.359	2.056	7.403	1.408
1986	4.666	3.617	7.403	1.009
1987	4.816	4.013	6.050	0.685
1988	5.360	4.660	6.500	0.584
1989	6.427	6.013	7.293	0.475
1990	5.959	5.603	6.480	0.301
1991	4.424	3.910	4.940	0.351
1992	2.828	2.128	3.615	0.468
1993	2.406	2.067	2.740	0.208
1994	2.827	2.056	4.185	0.628
1995	3.874	3.361	4.422	0.302

The Kenny Index is composed of high-grade securities issued by state, municipal, local and other government bodies. The interest income on these securities is exempt from federal income taxes but not necessarily from state or local income taxes. The Kenny S&P 30-day High Grade Index is a weekly reset index comprised of 34 MIG-1 rated issues. These issues are municipal tax exempt notes that are calculated on a 30/360 basis, and are not subject to alternative minimum tax (AMT). The coupon on each issue is adjusted to price that component at par for a theoretical 30-day maturity. The coupons are then averaged to derive the index.

The yields of the above index are substantially lower than yields on other short-term instruments, primarily because the index consists of tax-exempt securities.

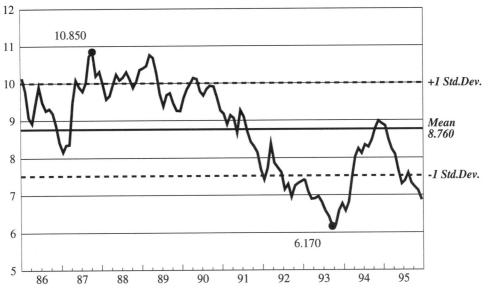

30 Year GNMA

Date Range	Mean	Min.	Max.	Std.Dev.
1986-1995	8.760	6.170	10.850	1.239
1986	9.316	8.410	10.144	0.481
1987	9.684	8.158	10.850	0.922
1988	10.030	9.572	10.356	0.238
1989	9.924	9.262	10.756	0.558
1990	9.809	9.276	10.141	0.242
1991	8.716	7.698	9.273	0.489
1992	7.519	6.954	8.378	0.396
1993	6.738	6.170	7.420	0.364
1994	8.083	6.579	8.976	0.768
1995	7.680	6.872	8.848	0.606

The mortgage pools underlying Government National Mortgage Association (GNMA) pass-through securities consist of FHA-insured or VA-guaranteed mortgage loans. GNMA, which is backed by the full faith and credit of the U.S. Government, in turn guarantees the timely payment of principal and interest on its securities. GNMA delays principal and interest payments by 45 days from the time they are received. The yield is expressed on a semi-annual bond equivalent basis for the current coupon. The average life of a GNMA pass-through is about 10 years, even though stated maturity may be longer.

SPREADS ANALYSIS

PART 1
Spreads Analysis

SECTION II
Money Market Based Spreads

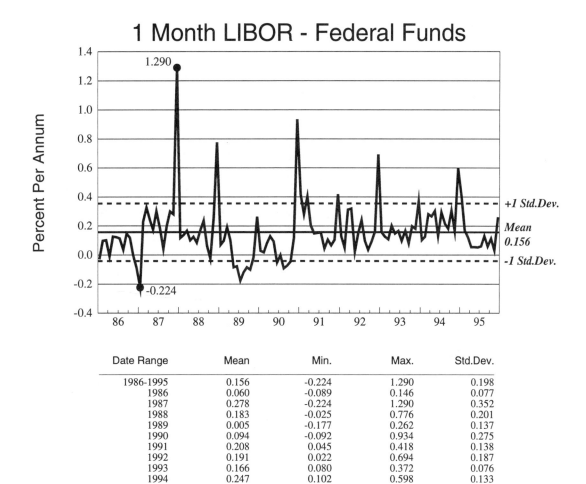

Date Range	Mean	Min.	Max.	Std.Dev.
1986-1995	0.156	-0.224	1.290	0.198
1986	0.060	-0.089	0.146	0.077
1987	0.278	-0.224	1.290	0.352
1988	0.183	-0.025	0.776	0.201
1989	0.005	-0.177	0.262	0.137
1990	0.094	-0.092	0.934	0.275
1991	0.208	0.045	0.418	0.138
1992	0.191	0.022	0.694	0.187
1993	0.166	0.080	0.372	0.076
1994	0.247	0.102	0.598	0.133
1995	0.124	0.031	0.393	0.107

The overnight Federal Funds rate is the rate at which banks borrow or lend money to and from each other overnight. It reflects the relative ease or tightness of U.S. credit market conditions. The above spread is positive when the short term U.S. yield curve is positively sloped. The magnitude of the spread is a function of the shape of the U.S. yield curve, short term interest rate expectations, and the absolute level of interest rates.

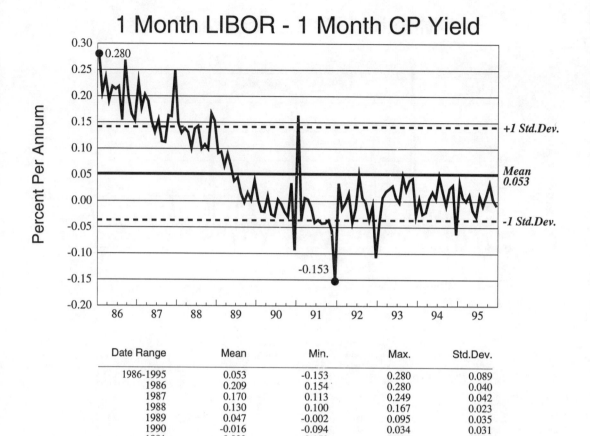

Date Range	Mean	Min.	Max.	Std.Dev.
1986-1995	0.053	-0.153	0.280	0.089
1986	0.209	0.154	0.280	0.040
1987	0.170	0.113	0.249	0.042
1988	0.130	0.100	0.167	0.023
1989	0.047	-0.002	0.095	0.035
1990	-0.016	-0.094	0.034	0.031
1991	-0.023	-0.153	0.164	0.071
1992	-0.010	-0.108	0.049	0.040
1993	0.014	-0.043	0.048	0.028
1994	0.003	-0.063	0.047	0.029
1995	0.004	-0.030	0.034	0.019

At identical maturities, the above spread results from the difference in issuer credit quality. The commercial paper market is dominated by top-rated firms which generally pay a rate substantially lower than the cost of funds in the Eurodollar market. Recently, the spread has narrowed, reflecting investors' increased concern about the credit quality of corporate issuers and decreased corporate demand for LIBOR-based loans.

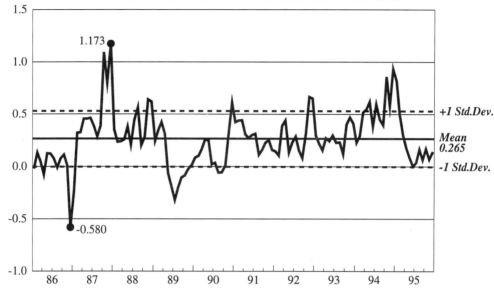

3 Month LIBOR - Federal Funds

Date Range	Mean	Min.	Max.	Std.Dev.
1986-1995	0.265	-0.580	1.173	0.266
1986	0.002	-0.580	0.134	0.195
1987	0.493	-0.233	1.173	0.378
1988	0.369	0.203	0.641	0.162
1989	0.030	-0.321	0.424	0.242
1990	0.146	-0.057	0.610	0.192
1991	0.284	0.113	0.440	0.110
1992	0.300	0.084	0.667	0.202
1993	0.278	0.120	0.469	0.104
1994	0.533	0.227	0.934	0.209
1995	0.212	0.003	0.817	0.233

The overnight Federal Funds rate is the rate at which banks borrow or lend money to and from each other overnight. The spread is a function of the shape of the U.S. yield curve at the short end and market perceptions of risk. The spread is positive when the U.S. yield curve is positively sloped, and negative when the yield curve inverts, typically prior to a recession.

SPREADS ANALYSIS

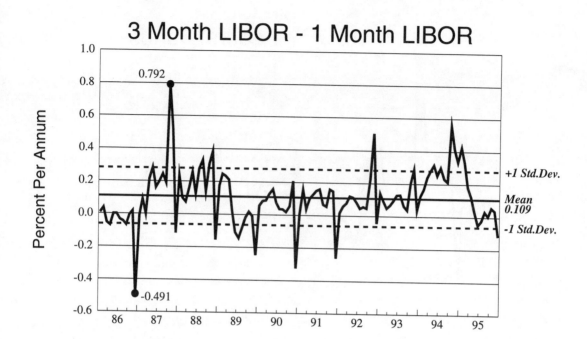

Date Range	Mean	Min.	Max.	Std.Dev.
1986-1995	0.109	-0.491	0.792	0.171
1986	-0.058	-0.491	0.037	0.140
1987	0.215	-0.117	0.792	0.245
1988	0.186	-0.155	0.385	0.146
1989	0.026	-0.246	0.247	0.161
1990	0.052	-0.324	0.208	0.130
1991	0.076	-0.259	0.161	0.118
1992	0.109	-0.043	0.507	0.141
1993	0.111	0.038	0.287	0.074
1994	0.286	0.125	0.554	0.114
1995	0.088	-0.116	0.424	0.157

The above spread is a function of the shape of the U.S. yield curve at the short end. The spread is positive when the U.S. yield curve is positively sloped, and negative when the U.S. yield curve inverts, typically prior to a recession.

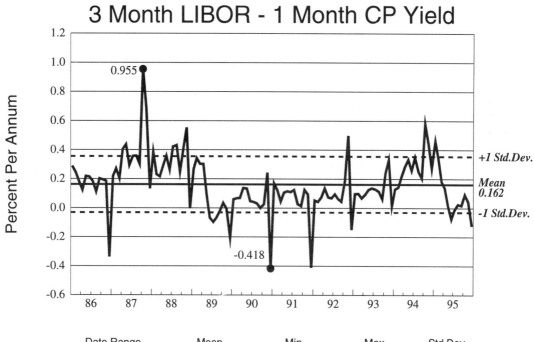

Date Range	Mean	Min.	Max.	Std.Dev.
1986-1995	0.162	-0.418	0.955	0.193
1986	0.151	-0.337	0.288	0.161
1987	0.384	0.132	0.955	0.228
1988	0.316	-0.002	0.552	0.142
1989	0.073	-0.206	0.342	0.186
1990	0.036	-0.418	0.242	0.157
1991	0.053	-0.412	0.170	0.153
1992	0.099	-0.151	0.498	0.149
1993	0.125	0.011	0.331	0.085
1994	0.288	0.129	0.578	0.126
1995	0.092	-0.125	0.458	0.168

The above spread has generally been positive primarily due to (1) the difference in issuer credit quality and (2) the shape of the yield curve at its short end. The commercial paper market is dominated by top-rated firms which generally pay a rate below the cost of funds in the Eurodollar market.

SPREADS ANALYSIS

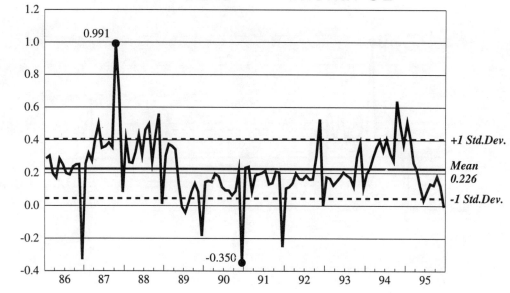

3 Month LIBOR - 1 Month CD

Date Range	Mean	Min.	Max.	Std.Dev.
1986-1995	0.226	-0.350	0.991	0.180
1986	0.192	-0.330	0.304	0.170
1987	0.415	0.083	0.991	0.232
1988	0.353	0.011	0.561	0.145
1989	0.135	-0.184	0.374	0.179
1990	0.095	-0.350	0.214	0.147
1991	0.149	-0.251	0.238	0.133
1992	0.186	0.001	0.527	0.128
1993	0.189	0.110	0.379	0.078
1994	0.360	0.197	0.639	0.119
1995	0.183	-0.006	0.507	0.150

The above spread is a function of 1) the shape of the U.S. yield curve at its short end; 2) FDIC insurance costs; and 3) reserve requirements for time deposits such as CDs (prior to December, 1990).

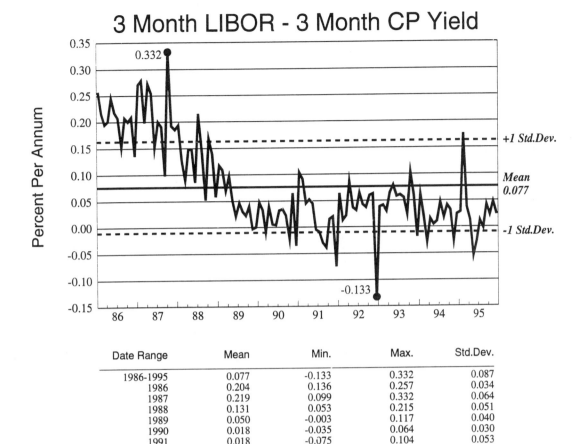

Date Range	Mean	Min.	Max.	Std.Dev.
1986-1995	0.077	-0.133	0.332	0.087
1986	0.204	0.136	0.257	0.034
1987	0.219	0.099	0.332	0.064
1988	0.131	0.053	0.215	0.051
1989	0.050	-0.003	0.117	0.040
1990	0.018	-0.035	0.064	0.030
1991	0.018	-0.075	0.104	0.053
1992	0.033	-0.133	0.087	0.056
1993	0.050	-0.018	0.103	0.030
1994	0.018	-0.028	0.061	0.027
1995	0.027	-0.055	0.176	0.055

At identical maturities, the above spread results from the difference in issuer credit quality. The commercial paper market is dominated by top-rated firms which generally pay a rate lower than the cost of funds in the Eurodollar market. Recently, the spread has narrowed, reflecting investors' increased concern about the credit quality of corporate issuers and decreased corporate demand for LIBOR-based loans.

SPREADS ANALYSIS

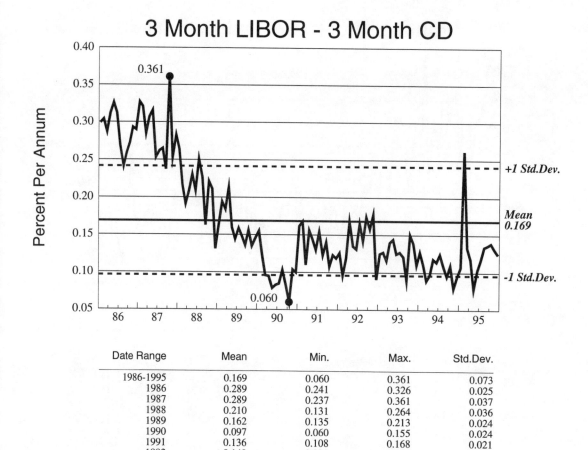

Date Range	Mean	Min.	Max.	Std.Dev.
1986-1995	0.169	0.060	0.361	0.073
1986	0.289	0.241	0.326	0.025
1987	0.289	0.237	0.361	0.037
1988	0.210	0.131	0.264	0.036
1989	0.162	0.135	0.213	0.024
1990	0.097	0.060	0.155	0.024
1991	0.136	0.108	0.168	0.021
1992	0.140	0.091	0.177	0.029
1993	0.126	0.090	0.150	0.016
1994	0.105	0.079	0.127	0.015
1995	0.132	0.078	0.262	0.045

At identical maturities, the above spread is a function of (1) FDIC insurance costs; and (2) reserve requirements for time deposits such as CDs (prior to December, 1990).

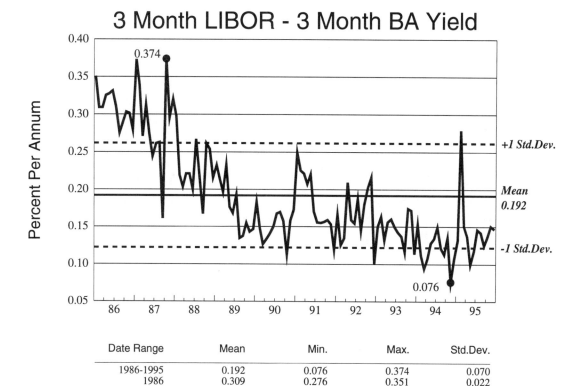

Date Range	Mean	Min.	Max.	Std.Dev.
1986-1995	0.192	0.076	0.374	0.070
1986	0.309	0.276	0.351	0.022
1987	0.291	0.161	0.374	0.059
1988	0.229	0.167	0.297	0.035
1989	0.177	0.135	0.233	0.036
1990	0.152	0.113	0.183	0.021
1991	0.183	0.120	0.249	0.040
1992	0.165	0.101	0.216	0.035
1993	0.147	0.114	0.174	0.020
1994	0.119	0.076	0.153	0.022
1995	0.147	0.099	0.279	0.044

At identical maturities, the spread between these two rates reflects their different credit quality. BAs are of superior credit quality because, in addition to being the irrevocable obligation of the accepting bank, they are also a contingent liability of the drawer of the draft. As a result, the spread between LIBOR and BA rates has been positive. As corporate demand for LIBOR-based bank loans has decreased, LIBOR rates and, hence, spreads between LIBOR and BA rates, have declined.

SPREADS ANALYSIS

Kenny Index As A Percentage Of 3 Month LIBOR*

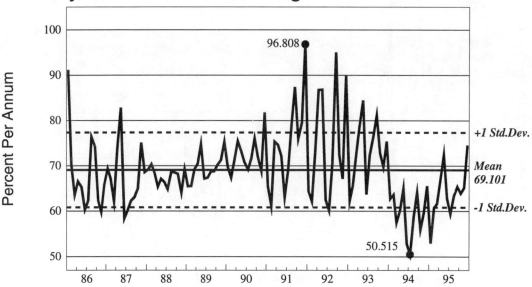

Date Range	Mean	Min.	Max.	Std.Dev.
1986-1995	69.101	50.515	96.808	8.259
1986	68.183	59.750	91.175	8.924
1987	67.322	58.390	82.809	7.085
1988	67.559	64.092	70.374	1.969
1989	69.543	65.503	75.242	3.129
1990	72.305	67.410	81.818	3.940
1991	75.018	61.254	96.808	10.136
1992	74.254	60.184	95.036	12.207
1993	72.960	62.343	84.464	6.827
1994	59.718	50.515	65.551	4.838
1995	64.145	52.959	74.586	5.706

* Kenny Index divided by 3 month LIBOR, stated as a percent.

The Kenny Index is composed of high-grade securities issued by state, municipal, local and other government bodies. The interest income on these securities is exempt from federal income taxes but not necessarily from state or local income taxes. Quoted weekly, the index is based on the average 30-day yield evaluations at par of not less than 20 component issues of notes, selected by Kenny Information Systems. The yield is calculated using actual number of days to maturity and a 365-day year.

The above spread is influenced by (1) differences in credit quality, (2) the shape of the yield curve at its short end, and (3) tax factors such as the marginal tax rate and federal tax reform, e.g., Tax Reform Act of 1986.

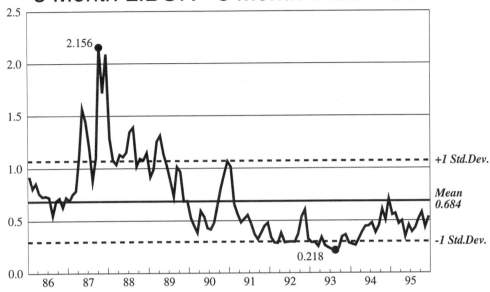

3 Month LIBOR - 3 Month T-Bill Yield

Date Range	Mean	Min.	Max.	Std.Dev.
1986-1995	0.684	0.218	2.156	0.386
1986	0.737	0.553	0.922	0.096
1987	1.290	0.692	2.156	0.506
1988	1.155	1.020	1.389	0.121
1989	0.967	0.684	1.312	0.205
1990	0.608	0.387	1.064	0.221
1991	0.522	0.321	1.014	0.180
1992	0.360	0.288	0.602	0.104
1993	0.280	0.218	0.365	0.049
1994	0.441	0.264	0.704	0.128
1995	0.482	0.346	0.578	0.073

At identical maturities, the above spread reflects the superior credit quality of T-Bills, a U.S. government obligation, and their exemption from state and local income taxes.

SPREADS ANALYSIS

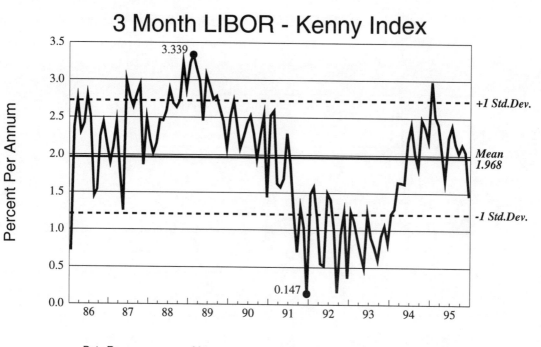

Date Range	Mean	Min.	Max.	Std.Dev.
1986-1995	1.968	0.147	3.339	0.758
1986	2.141	0.717	2.795	0.606
1987	2.334	1.256	2.993	0.544
1988	2.578	2.019	3.229	0.343
1989	2.820	2.096	3.339	0.369
1990	2.286	1.440	2.719	0.338
1991	1.547	0.147	2.591	0.729
1992	0.994	0.164	1.576	0.487
1993	0.894	0.504	1.248	0.233
1994	1.908	1.222	2.475	0.431
1995	2.174	1.460	2.986	0.393

The Kenny Index is composed of high-grade securities issued by state, municipal, local and other government bodies. The interest income on these securities is exempt from federal income taxes but not necessarily from state or local income taxes. The Kenny S&P 30-day High Grade Index is a weekly reset index comprised of 34 MIG-1 rated issues. These issues are municipal tax exempt notes that are calculated on a 30/360 basis, and are not subject to alternative minimum tax (AMT). The coupon on each issue is adjusted to price that component at par for a theoretical 30-day maturity. The coupons are then averaged to derive the index.

The above spread, which compares short-term tax-exempt and taxable yields, is a function of (1) the shape of the yield curve at the short end; (2) credit differences between high-grade government obligations and those of Eurodollar issuers; and (3) tax factors such as the marginal tax rate and anticipated federal tax reform.

SPREADS ANALYSIS

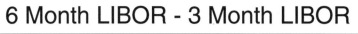

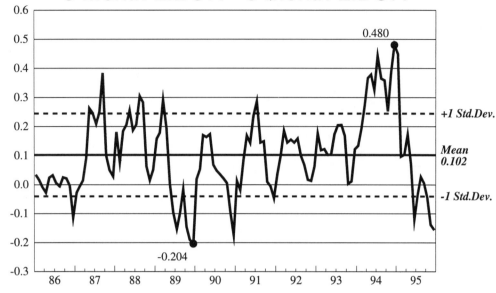

Date Range	Mean	Min.	Max.	Std.Dev.
1986-1995	0.102	-0.204	0.480	0.143
1986	-0.000	-0.114	0.034	0.040
1987	0.134	-0.028	0.384	0.132
1988	0.168	0.015	0.304	0.095
1989	-0.007	-0.204	0.291	0.171
1990	0.041	-0.173	0.174	0.103
1991	0.097	-0.047	0.286	0.108
1992	0.099	0.013	0.185	0.059
1993	0.126	0.003	0.205	0.066
1994	0.329	0.134	0.480	0.100
1995	0.036	-0.156	0.448	0.166

The above spread is largely a function of the shape of the U.S. yield curve at its short end. It is positive when the U.S. yield curve is positively sloped and negative when the U.S. yield curve inverts, typically prior to a recession.

SPREADS ANALYSIS

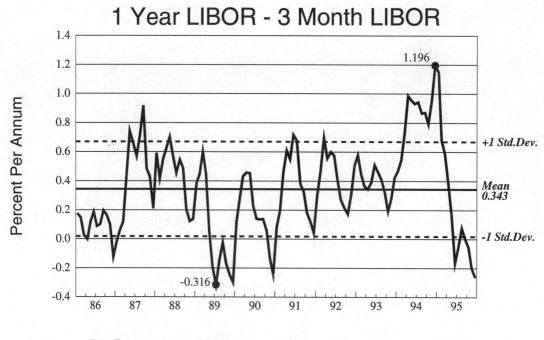

Date Range	Mean	Min.	Max.	Std.Dev.
1986-1995	0.343	-0.316	1.196	0.326
1986	0.098	-0.123	0.195	0.093
1987	0.444	-0.013	0.917	0.297
1988	0.451	0.122	0.703	0.195
1989	0.046	-0.316	0.601	0.333
1990	0.172	-0.244	0.458	0.220
1991	0.361	0.042	0.716	0.240
1992	0.423	0.173	0.696	0.168
1993	0.393	0.190	0.578	0.104
1994	0.853	0.470	1.196	0.198
1995	0.194	-0.263	1.147	0.428

The above spread is a function of the shape of the U.S. yield curve at its short end.

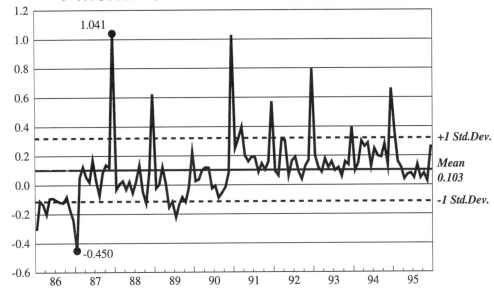

Date Range	Mean	Min.	Max.	Std.Dev.
1986-1995	0.103	-0.450	1.041	0.217
1986	-0.149	-0.309	-0.082	0.070
1987	0.108	-0.450	1.041	0.336
1988	0.053	-0.125	0.623	0.192
1989	-0.043	-0.223	0.222	0.124
1990	0.110	-0.086	1.028	0.297
1991	0.231	0.087	0.571	0.138
1992	0.202	0.039	0.802	0.209
1993	0.153	0.058	0.399	0.087
1994	0.244	0.098	0.661	0.148
1995	0.120	0.028	0.359	0.101

The above spread is a function of (1) the difference in credit quality between these two instruments and (2) the shape of the yield curve at the short end. The commercial paper market is dominated by top-rated firms which typically pay a rate below the cost of overnight interbank borrowing. During recessions and periods of weak economic activity, the yield on quality paper (CP) generally declines in relation to other money market instruments, reducing the spread. During periods of recovery and growth, the spread nudges closer to zero or turns positive.

SPREADS ANALYSIS

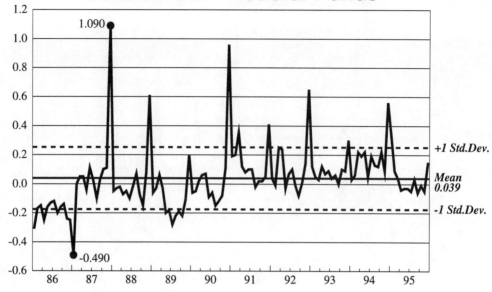

Date Range	Mean	Min.	Max.	Std.Dev.
1986-1995	0.039	-0.490	1.090	0.214
1986	-0.190	-0.310	-0.120	0.060
1987	0.078	-0.490	1.090	0.358
1988	0.017	-0.150	0.610	0.197
1989	-0.105	-0.280	0.200	0.139
1990	0.051	-0.150	0.960	0.297
1991	0.135	-0.020	0.410	0.132
1992	0.114	-0.080	0.650	0.198
1993	0.089	0.000	0.300	0.076
1994	0.173	0.030	0.560	0.140
1995	0.029	-0.060	0.310	0.109

The above spread is a function of the shape of the yield curve, the status of the business cycle and interest rate expectations.

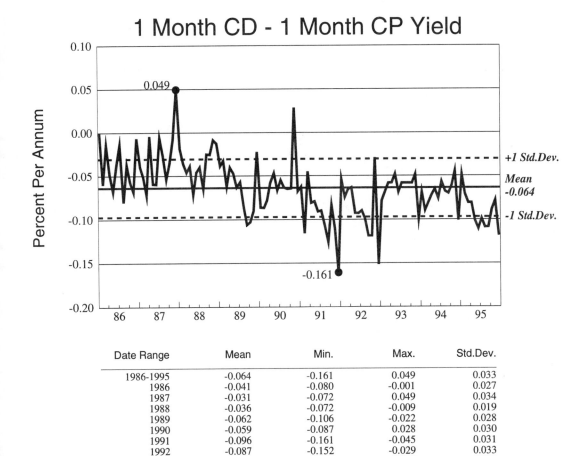

Date Range	Mean	Min.	Max.	Std.Dev.
1986-1995	-0.064	-0.161	0.049	0.033
1986	-0.041	-0.080	-0.001	0.027
1987	-0.031	-0.072	0.049	0.034
1988	-0.036	-0.072	-0.009	0.019
1989	-0.062	-0.106	-0.022	0.028
1990	-0.059	-0.087	0.028	0.030
1991	-0.096	-0.161	-0.045	0.031
1992	-0.087	-0.152	-0.029	0.033
1993	-0.063	-0.099	-0.048	0.014
1994	-0.071	-0.101	-0.044	0.015
1995	-0.091	-0.119	-0.049	0.020

Unlike CP, most CDs are FDIC-insured. For identical maturities, the above spread is generally negative. The spread tends to widen when confidence in the financial market is shaken by bank defaults and liquidations, compelling banks to offer higher rates on CDs. Prior to December, 1990, the spread also reflects reserve requirements for time deposits such as CDs.

SPREADS ANALYSIS

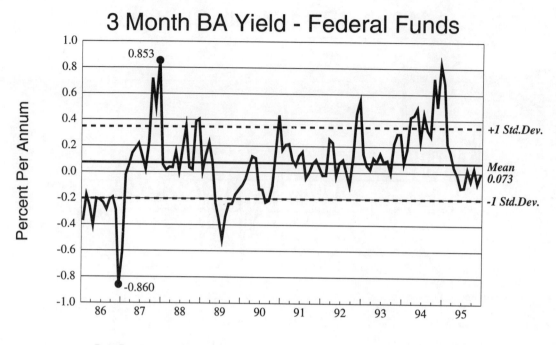

Date Range	Mean	Min.	Max.	Std.Dev.
1986-1995	0.073	-0.860	0.853	0.274
1986	-0.307	-0.860	-0.175	0.188
1987	0.202	-0.606	0.853	0.375
1988	0.141	0.009	0.405	0.155
1989	-0.147	-0.514	0.228	0.220
1990	-0.006	-0.227	0.437	0.191
1991	0.101	-0.042	0.219	0.081
1992	0.135	-0.096	0.550	0.201
1993	0.131	0.004	0.297	0.097
1994	0.414	0.074	0.827	0.214
1995	0.065	-0.115	0.685	0.219

The spread is a function of (1) the shape of the yield curve at the short end, and (2) the superior credit quality of BAs which, in addition to being the irrevocable obligation of the accepting bank, are also the contingent liability of the drawer of the draft (versus the Federal Funds rate which is the overnight interbank borrowing rate).

3 Month BA Yield - 1 Month CP Yield

Date Range	Mean	Min.	Max.	Std.Dev.
1986-1995	-0.030	-0.617	0.581	0.177
1986	-0.159	-0.617	-0.063	0.149
1987	0.093	-0.188	0.581	0.219
1988	0.088	-0.217	0.298	0.127
1989	-0.105	-0.353	0.127	0.159
1990	-0.116	-0.590	0.084	0.165
1991	-0.130	-0.531	-0.032	0.134
1992	-0.067	-0.252	0.282	0.124
1993	-0.022	-0.103	0.159	0.071
1994	0.169	-0.024	0.443	0.130
1995	-0.055	-0.271	0.326	0.153

The spread is a function of (1) the shape of the yield curve at the short end, and (2) the superior credit quality of BAs which, in addition to being the irrevocable obligation of the accepting bank, are also the contingent liability of the drawer of the draft (versus commercial paper of high quality corporate issuers).

SPREADS ANALYSIS

PART 1
Spreads Analysis

SECTION III
Treasury Based Spreads

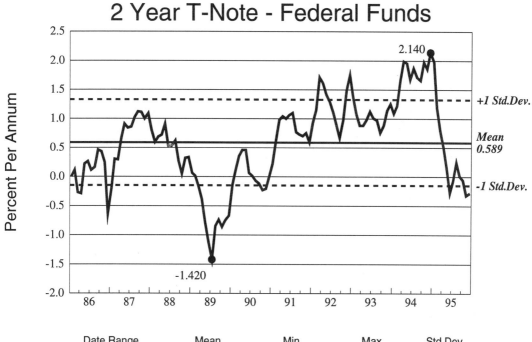

Date Range	Mean	Min.	Max.	Std.Dev.
1986-1995	0.589	-1.420	2.140	0.740
1986	0.066	-0.640	0.460	0.321
1987	0.749	-0.200	1.120	0.414
1988	0.530	0.050	0.910	0.248
1989	-0.641	-1.420	0.060	0.444
1990	0.058	-0.230	0.460	0.245
1991	0.798	0.220	1.100	0.255
1992	1.249	0.670	1.750	0.350
1993	1.026	0.760	1.370	0.174
1994	1.734	1.090	2.140	0.311
1995	0.324	-0.320	1.980	0.697

The spread is a function of (1) the shape of the yield curve and (2) the difference in credit quality between Treasury notes, U.S. government obligations, and overnight Federal Funds, which are unsecured interbank borrowings. In general, changes in the Federal Funds rate are quickly reflected in Treasury Note yields since the Fed Funds rate is a barometer of money market rates.

SPREADS ANALYSIS

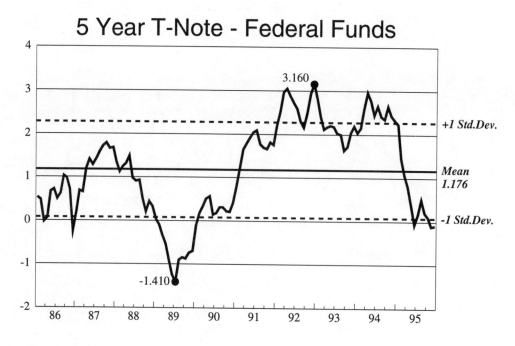

5 Year T-Note - Federal Funds

Date Range	Mean	Min.	Max.	Std.Dev.
1986-1995	1.176	-1.410	3.160	1.099
1986	0.506	-0.240	1.030	0.389
1987	1.278	0.210	1.790	0.502
1988	0.903	0.210	1.490	0.435
1989	-0.713	-1.410	0.030	0.425
1990	0.271	-0.110	0.560	0.179
1991	1.683	0.790	2.090	0.357
1992	2.667	2.160	3.160	0.339
1993	2.125	1.640	2.810	0.300
1994	2.482	2.040	2.960	0.258
1995	0.554	-0.110	2.230	0.720

The spread is a function of (1) the shape of the yield curve and (2) the difference in credit quality between Treasury notes, U.S. government obligations, and overnight Federal Funds, which are unsecured interbank borrowings. In general, changes in the Federal Funds rate are quickly reflected in Treasury Note yields since the Fed Funds rate is a barometer of money market rates.

SPREADS ANALYSIS

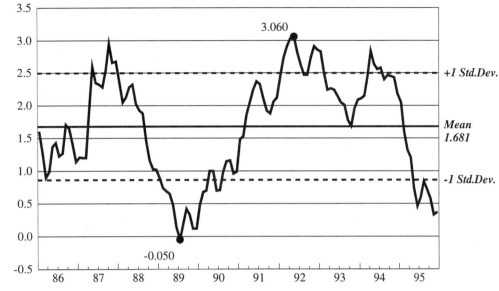

Date Range	Mean	Min.	Max.	Std.Dev.
1986-1995	1.681	-0.050	3.060	0.816
1986	1.333	0.900	1.710	0.252
1987	2.160	1.200	2.950	0.629
1988	1.804	1.020	2.370	0.505
1989	0.393	-0.050	0.880	0.298
1990	0.877	0.480	1.160	0.214
1991	1.995	1.480	2.370	0.280
1992	2.757	2.440	3.060	0.215
1993	2.150	1.690	2.830	0.306
1994	2.437	2.110	2.840	0.212
1995	0.901	0.330	2.050	0.535

Since the instruments only differ in maturity, the spread is a function of the shape of the U.S. yield curve. It is positive when the yield curve is positively sloped but narrows or turns negative when the yield curve inverts, typically prior to a recession.

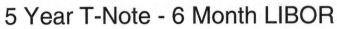

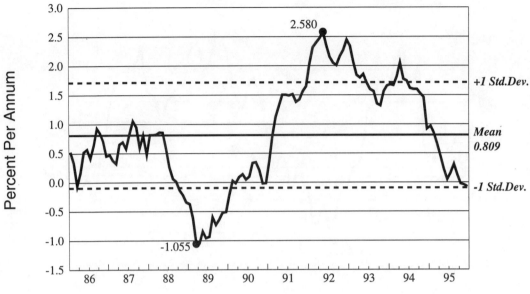

Date Range	Mean	Min.	Max.	Std.Dev.
1986-1995	0.809	-1.055	2.580	0.906
1986	0.504	-0.058	0.926	0.275
1987	0.651	0.321	1.055	0.227
1988	0.366	-0.342	0.857	0.473
1989	-0.736	-1.055	-0.374	0.227
1990	0.084	-0.215	0.344	0.157
1991	1.301	0.355	1.648	0.375
1992	2.268	2.008	2.580	0.189
1993	1.721	1.317	2.339	0.287
1994	1.619	0.916	2.047	0.268
1995	0.307	-0.078	0.965	0.355

The spread is a function of (1) the shape of the yield curve; (2) the difference in credit quality between Treasury bills, U.S. government obligations, and 6-month LIBOR, which is the cost of unsecured funds in the Eurodollar market; and (3) Treasury Notes' exemption from state and local income taxes.

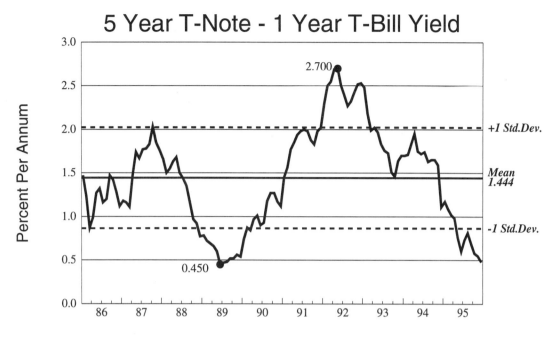

Date Range	Mean	Min.	Max.	Std.Dev.
1986-1995	1.444	0.450	2.700	0.580
1986	1.233	0.870	1.470	0.183
1987	1.613	1.110	2.030	0.307
1988	1.344	0.770	1.680	0.313
1989	0.582	0.450	0.780	0.107
1990	1.023	0.740	1.270	0.176
1991	1.853	1.450	2.020	0.181
1992	2.474	2.270	2.700	0.141
1993	1.856	1.460	2.480	0.290
1994	1.669	1.110	1.950	0.201
1995	0.788	0.480	1.170	0.228

Since the instruments only differ in maturity, the spread is a function of the shape of the U.S. yield curve. It is positive when the yield curve is positively sloped but narrows or turns negative when the yield curve inverts, typically prior to a recession.

SPREADS ANALYSIS

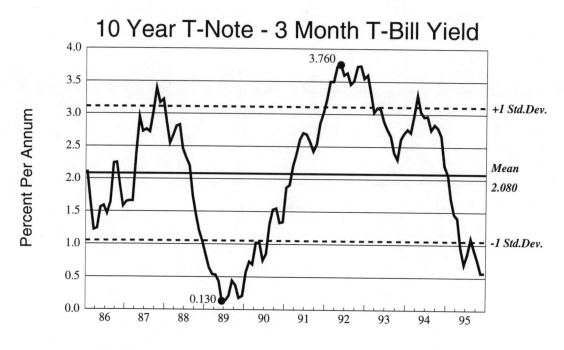

Date Range	Mean	Min.	Max.	Std.Dev.
1986-1995	2.080	0.130	3.760	1.029
1986	1.704	1.220	2.250	0.351
1987	2.609	1.650	3.390	0.633
1988	2.178	1.040	2.860	0.657
1989	0.387	0.130	0.820	0.220
1990	1.057	0.570	1.550	0.344
1991	2.483	1.870	3.020	0.350
1992	3.578	3.230	3.760	0.154
1993	2.876	2.310	3.600	0.373
1994	2.833	2.210	3.290	0.261
1995	1.090	0.570	2.070	0.475

Since the instruments only differ in maturity, the above spread is a function of the shape of the U.S. yield curve. It is positive when the yield curve is positively sloped but narrows or turns negative when the yield curve inverts, typically prior to a recession.

10 Year T-Note - 6 Month LIBOR

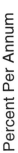

Date Range	Mean	Min.	Max.	Std.Dev.
1986-1995	1.208	-1.205	3.280	1.139
1986	0.876	0.262	1.456	0.374
1987	1.101	0.781	1.495	0.230
1988	0.741	-0.322	1.387	0.628
1989	-0.742	-1.205	-0.422	0.268
1990	0.264	-0.125	0.724	0.271
1991	1.790	0.745	2.548	0.489
1992	3.090	2.819	3.280	0.114
1993	2.447	1.937	3.109	0.356
1994	2.016	0.946	2.497	0.405
1995	0.496	0.122	0.985	0.301

The spread is a function of (1) the shape of the yield curve; (2) the difference in credit quality between Treasury bills, U.S. government obligations, and 6-month LIBOR which is the cost of unsecured funds in the Eurodollar market; and (3) Treasury notes' exemption from state and local income taxes.

SPREADS ANALYSIS

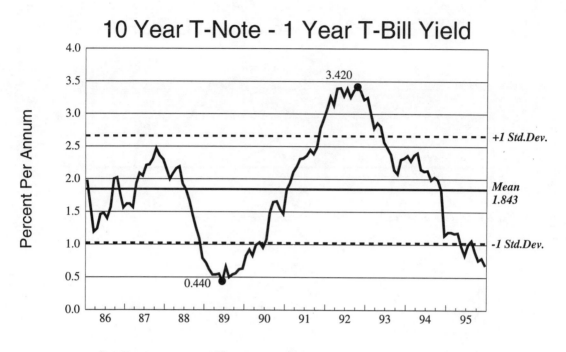

Date Range	Mean	Min.	Max.	Std.Dev.
1986-1995	1.843	0.440	3.420	0.820
1986	1.605	1.190	2.020	0.283
1987	2.063	1.570	2.470	0.312
1988	1.718	0.790	2.190	0.469
1989	0.577	0.440	0.720	0.076
1990	1.203	0.830	1.660	0.329
1991	2.342	1.840	2.920	0.310
1992	3.296	3.080	3.420	0.109
1993	2.582	2.080	3.250	0.362
1994	2.066	1.140	2.400	0.341
1995	0.977	0.680	1.190	0.184

Since the instruments only differ in maturity, the above spread is a function of the shape of the U.S. yield curve. It is positive when the yield curve is positively sloped but narrows or turns negative when the yield curve inverts, typically prior to a recession.

Date Range	Mean	Min.	Max.	Std.Dev.
1986-1995	0.985	-0.320	2.530	0.711
1986	0.812	0.570	1.150	0.211
1987	0.977	0.830	1.170	0.130
1988	0.748	0.020	1.130	0.365
1989	-0.078	-0.320	0.200	0.151
1990	0.393	-0.040	0.840	0.352
1991	1.373	0.960	2.060	0.349
1992	2.239	1.850	2.530	0.207
1993	1.825	1.460	2.210	0.278
1994	1.144	0.220	1.610	0.373
1995	0.419	0.270	0.510	0.072

Since the instruments only differ in maturity, the spread is a function of the shape of the U.S. yield curve. It is positive when the yield curve is positively sloped but narrows or turns negative when the yield curve inverts, typically prior to a recession.

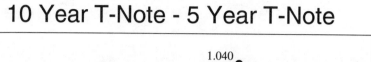

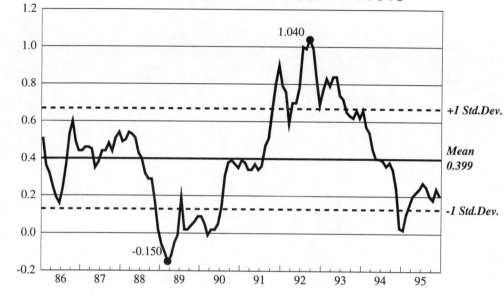

Date Range	Mean	Min.	Max.	Std.Dev.
1986-1995	0.399	-0.150	1.040	0.270
1986	0.372	0.160	0.600	0.144
1987	0.449	0.350	0.540	0.051
1988	0.374	0.020	0.540	0.162
1989	-0.006	-0.150	0.190	0.097
1990	0.180	-0.010	0.390	0.164
1991	0.488	0.340	0.900	0.194
1992	0.822	0.590	1.040	0.149
1993	0.726	0.620	0.840	0.088
1994	0.397	0.030	0.660	0.161
1995	0.189	0.020	0.270	0.071

Since the instruments only differ in maturity, the spread is a function of the shape of the U.S. yield curve. It is positive when the yield curve is positively sloped but narrows or turns negative when the yield curve inverts, typically prior to a recession.

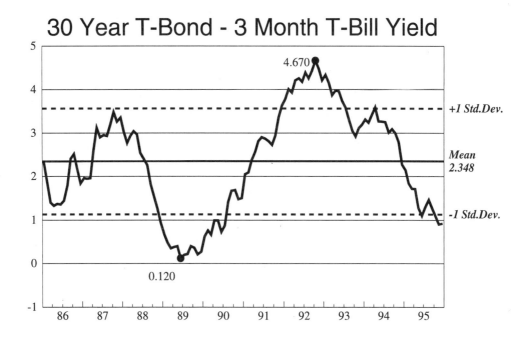

Date Range	Mean	Min.	Max.	Std.Dev.
1986-1995	2.348	0.120	4.670	1.218
1986	1.820	1.330	2.520	0.447
1987	2.805	1.950	3.480	0.560
1988	2.292	0.940	3.040	0.735
1989	0.338	0.120	0.660	0.146
1990	1.115	0.620	1.690	0.407
1991	2.761	2.050	3.630	0.460
1992	4.235	3.780	4.670	0.246
1993	3.601	2.920	4.340	0.476
1994	3.123	2.270	3.590	0.341
1995	1.394	0.900	2.140	0.387

Since the instruments only differ in maturity, the spread is a function of the shape of the U.S. yield curve. It is positive when the yield curve is positively sloped but narrows or turns negative when the yield curve inverts, typically prior to a recession.

SPREADS ANALYSIS

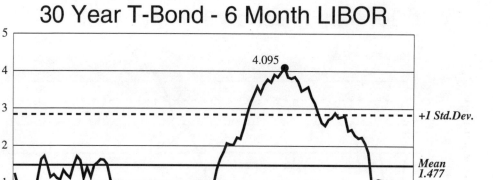

Date Range	Mean	Min.	Max.	Std.Dev.
1986-1995	1.477	-1.395	4.095	1.363
1986	0.992	0.442	1.717	0.470
1987	1.296	1.081	1.705	0.206
1988	0.854	-0.422	1.625	0.714
1989	-0.791	-1.395	-0.362	0.322
1990	0.323	-0.075	0.864	0.332
1991	2.067	0.925	3.158	0.609
1992	3.746	3.369	4.095	0.215
1993	3.172	2.547	3.849	0.460
1994	2.306	1.006	2.879	0.524
1995	0.800	0.472	1.091	0.229

The spread is a function of (1) the shape of the yield curve; (2) the difference in credit quality between Treasury bonds, U.S. government obligations, and LIBOR which is the cost of unsecured funds in the Eurodollar market; and (3) Treasury bonds' exemption from state and local income taxes.

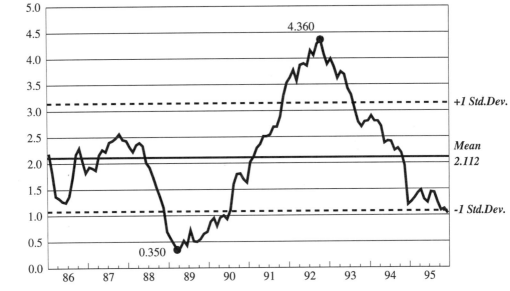

Date Range	Mean	Min.	Max.	Std.Dev.
1986-1995	2.112	0.350	4.360	1.034
1986	1.721	1.250	2.290	0.392
1987	2.258	1.870	2.560	0.243
1988	1.832	0.690	2.390	0.552
1989	0.528	0.350	0.720	0.115
1990	1.261	0.800	1.800	0.399
1991	2.619	2.020	3.530	0.443
1992	3.953	3.570	4.360	0.243
1993	3.307	2.690	3.990	0.473
1994	2.356	1.200	2.900	0.464
1995	1.282	1.030	1.480	0.147

Since the instruments only differ in maturity, the spread is a function of the shape of the U.S. yield curve. It is positive when the yield curve is positively sloped but narrows or turns negative when the yield curve inverts, typically prior to a recession.

SPREADS ANALYSIS

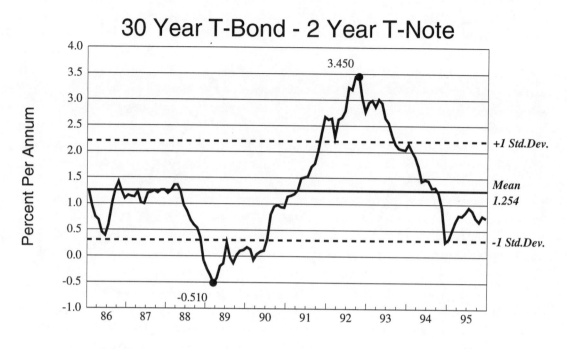

Date Range	Mean	Min.	Max.	Std.Dev.
1986-1995	1.254	-0.510	3.450	0.950
1986	0.927	0.390	1.420	0.346
1987	1.173	1.000	1.260	0.088
1988	0.861	-0.080	1.360	0.453
1989	-0.127	-0.510	0.260	0.234
1990	0.451	-0.070	0.980	0.426
1991	1.651	1.140	2.670	0.488
1992	2.896	2.280	3.450	0.372
1993	2.550	2.040	3.010	0.403
1994	1.434	0.280	2.150	0.507
1995	0.723	0.340	0.940	0.166

Since the instruments only differ in maturity, the spread is a function of the shape of the U.S. yield curve. It is positive when the yield curve is positively sloped but narrows or turns negative when the yield curve inverts, typically prior to a recession.

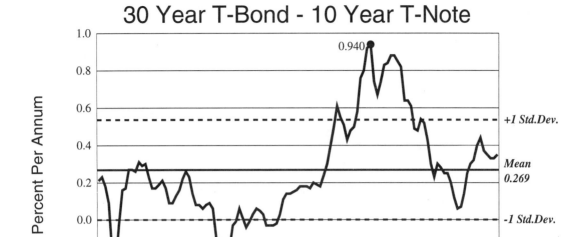

Date Range	Mean	Min.	Max.	Std.Dev.
1986-1995	0.269	-0.230	0.940	0.268
1986	0.116	-0.230	0.270	0.174
1987	0.196	0.090	0.310	0.076
1988	0.113	-0.100	0.260	0.097
1989	-0.049	-0.190	0.060	0.091
1990	0.058	-0.030	0.160	0.077
1991	0.278	0.170	0.610	0.148
1992	0.657	0.430	0.940	0.174
1993	0.725	0.480	0.880	0.148
1994	0.290	0.060	0.540	0.145
1995	0.304	0.070	0.440	0.106

Since the instruments only differ in maturity, the spread is a function of the shape of the U.S. yield curve. It is positive when the yield curve is positively sloped but narrows or turns negative when the yield curve inverts, typically prior to a recession.

SPREADS ANALYSIS

PART 1
Spreads Analysis

SECTION IV
Other Spreads

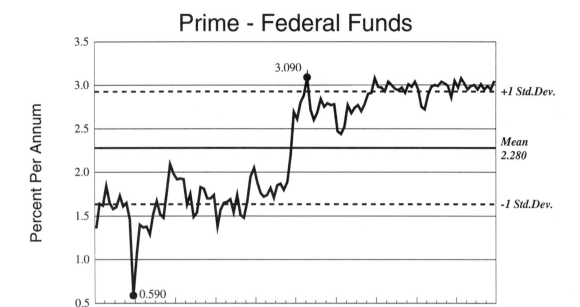

Date Range	Mean	Min.	Max.	Std.Dev.
1986-1995	2.280	0.590	3.090	0.646
1986	1.528	0.590	1.840	0.319
1987	1.546	1.070	2.090	0.291
1988	1.747	1.490	1.930	0.145
1989	1.657	1.380	2.050	0.191
1990	1.910	1.710	2.690	0.277
1991	2.776	2.600	3.090	0.130
1992	2.730	2.440	3.080	0.188
1993	2.978	2.910	3.040	0.040
1994	2.937	2.720	3.050	0.110
1995	2.993	2.950	3.080	0.042

Changes in the Prime rate tend to track changes in Federal Funds. Variations in spreads between Prime and other money market rates increase and the average levels of these spreads widen during periods of overall rate volatility and when the risks accompanying Prime-based loans increase.

SPREADS ANALYSIS

Prime - 1 Month CP Yield

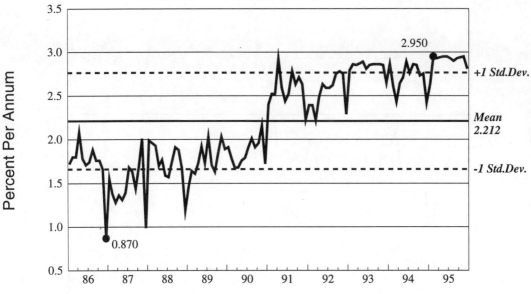

Date Range	Mean	Min.	Max.	Std.Dev.
1986-1995	2.212	0.870	2.950	0.551
1986	1.713	0.870	2.080	0.286
1987	1.476	0.990	2.010	0.259
1988	1.743	1.190	1.990	0.225
1989	1.769	1.470	2.030	0.175
1990	1.856	1.680	2.160	0.146
1991	2.574	2.230	2.920	0.182
1992	2.540	2.220	2.780	0.186
1993	2.833	2.650	2.890	0.063
1994	2.709	2.420	2.890	0.159
1995	2.902	2.640	2.950	0.091

Changes in the Prime rate tend to track changes in Federal Funds. Variations in spreads between Prime and other money market rates increase and average spread levels widen during periods of overall rate volatility and when the risks accompanying Prime-based loans increase. In recent years, the bulk of corporate credit has been priced from indices other than the Prime rate and Prime has developed as a basis for consumer loans, such as credit cards.

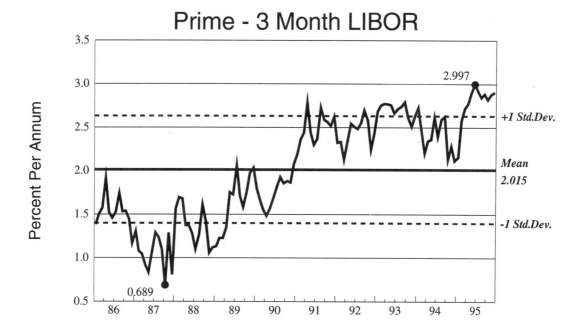

Date Range	Mean	Min.	Max.	Std.Dev.
1986-1995	2.015	0.689	2.997	0.617
1986	1.526	1.170	1.918	0.181
1987	1.053	0.689	1.303	0.206
1988	1.377	1.059	1.694	0.223
1989	1.627	1.134	2.061	0.326
1990	1.765	1.485	2.080	0.175
1991	2.492	2.188	2.784	0.176
1992	2.430	2.131	2.696	0.161
1993	2.700	2.511	2.790	0.083
1994	2.404	2.116	2.723	0.203
1995	2.781	2.153	2.997	0.226

Changes in the Prime rate tend to track changes in Federal Funds, while LIBOR responds almost instantaneously to fluctuations in U.S. domestic money market rates. The Prime rate's lagged behavior has affected both the level and the volatility of this spread. In recent years, the bulk of corporate credit has been priced from indices other than the Prime rate and Prime has developed as a basis for consumer loans, such as credit cards.

SPREADS ANALYSIS

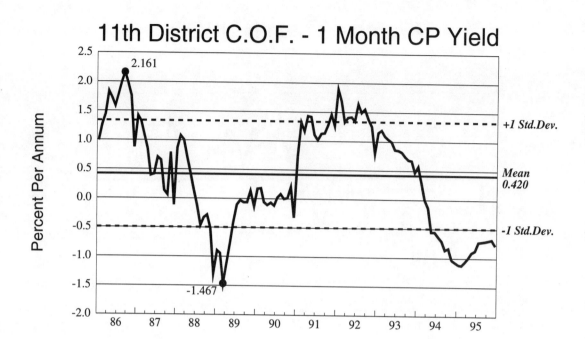

Date Range	Mean	Min.	Max.	Std.Dev.
1986-1995	0.420	-1.467	2.161	0.916
1986	1.616	0.879	2.161	0.401
1987	0.645	-0.115	1.419	0.489
1988	0.106	-1.290	1.080	0.731
1989	-0.491	-1.467	0.130	0.527
1990	-0.002	-0.320	0.200	0.149
1991	1.208	0.740	1.460	0.203
1992	1.434	0.798	1.890	0.268
1993	0.881	0.472	1.193	0.219
1994	-0.404	-1.033	0.570	0.515
1995	-0.865	-1.125	-0.681	0.171

The 11th District Cost of Funds Index is the monthly weighted average cost of funds of the 11th District (Federal Home Loan Banks) savings and loan associations (S&Ls). While most S&L deposits are FDIC-insured, commercial paper is an unsecured instrument issued by top-rated firms. Government regulations had artificially kept the cost of funds for S&Ls below market levels until deregulation in December, 1982, drove up S&Ls' cost of funds.

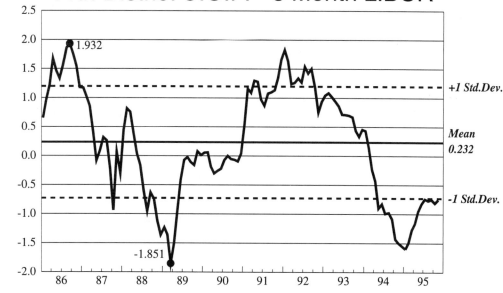

11th District C.O.F. - 3 Month LIBOR

Date Range	Mean	Min.	Max.	Std.Dev.
1986-1995	0.232	-1.851	1.932	0.964
1986	1.428	0.651	1.932	0.378
1987	0.223	-0.937	1.172	0.599
1988	-0.259	-1.361	0.814	0.745
1989	-0.634	-1.851	0.075	0.699
1990	-0.093	-0.305	0.058	0.125
1991	1.125	0.528	1.661	0.277
1992	1.324	0.751	1.824	0.293
1993	0.747	0.333	1.086	0.251
1994	-0.710	-1.502	0.433	0.620
1995	-1.014	-1.600	-0.743	0.319

The 11th District Cost of Funds Index is the monthly weighted average cost of funds of the 11th District (Federal Home Loan Banks) savings and loan associations (S&Ls). While most S&L deposits are FDIC-insured, LIBOR rates are for unsecured Eurodollar borrowings which are not subject to the same requirements as domestic deposits. Government regulations had artificially kept the cost of funds for S&Ls below market levels until deregulation in December, 1982, drove up S&Ls' cost of funds. The generally positive spread is largely a function of the instruments' credit quality, partially offset by maturity differences.

Eurodollar deposits are not subject to reserve requirements, taxation, and FDIC insurance premiums that affect U.S. domestic deposits. As a result, the yield on Eurodollar deposits is sometimes higher than the cost of deposits to the S&Ls.

SPREADS ANALYSIS

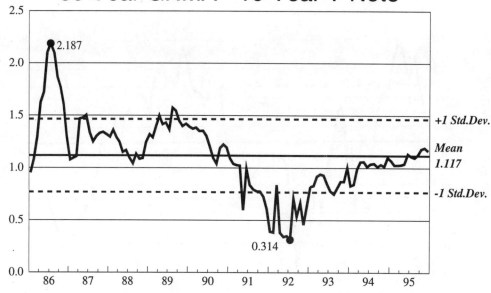

30 Year GNMA - 10 Year T-Note

Date Range	Mean	Min.	Max.	Std.Dev.
1986-1995	1.117	0.314	2.187	0.349
1986	1.634	0.954	2.187	0.406
1987	1.300	1.078	1.504	0.147
1988	1.185	1.043	1.362	0.101
1989	1.426	1.291	1.573	0.084
1990	1.259	1.040	1.392	0.118
1991	0.858	0.597	1.093	0.173
1992	0.487	0.314	0.838	0.175
1993	0.865	0.750	1.004	0.073
1994	1.003	0.829	1.100	0.083
1995	1.100	1.027	1.192	0.061

Although GNMAs and T-Notes are of similar credit quality, GNMAs carry prepayment risk and therefore trade at a positive spread to Treasuries. During 1986 and 1993, prepayments increased dramatically on all mortgage-backed securities, causing the GNMA-to-Treasury spread to widen significantly.

PART 1
Spreads Analysis

SECTION V
Corporate Bond Spreads

Corporate Bond Spreads: Industrials AAA-Aaa

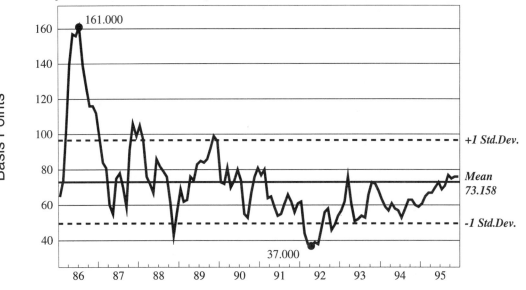

Date Range	Mean	Min.	Max.	Std.Dev.
1986-1995	73.158	37.000	161.000	23.441
1986	122.250	65.000	161.000	31.025
1987	79.583	55.000	106.000	16.670
1988	75.083	43.000	105.000	17.053
1989	80.750	62.000	99.000	12.159
1990	71.333	53.000	81.000	9.168
1991	63.333	54.000	80.000	8.072
1992	47.333	37.000	62.000	8.606
1993	62.083	51.000	76.000	8.847
1994	59.250	53.000	63.000	2.989
1995	70.583	61.000	77.000	5.017

The basic characteristics of corporate bonds are similar to those of U.S. Treasury bonds: fixed face values, interest paid semi-annually, and standard denominations of $1,000. Corporate bonds are sold to yield at a spread over Treasuries, which is determined by factors such as tenor, credit risk of the issuer, the current and anticipated supply of new issues, expectations for interest rates and the economy, and the presence of embedded options. Similar factors affect secondary market spreads, as well as the expected remaining life of the issue. Spreads may diverge for bonds with embedded options, as the securities may trade at yields that reflect the expectation that the issue will be called or refunded before maturity. The bonds comprising our data set are rated "Aaa" by Moody's and have an average remaining life of 27 years. A time series of spread levels and changes for similarly-rated bonds with shorter remaining lives would behave differently over time. The "Aaa" (Moody's) or "AAA" (Standard & Poor's) ratings are assigned to bonds of the highest quality, indicating exceptional potential to meet all interest and principal payments.

SPREADS ANALYSIS

Corporate Bond Spreads: Industrials AA-Aa

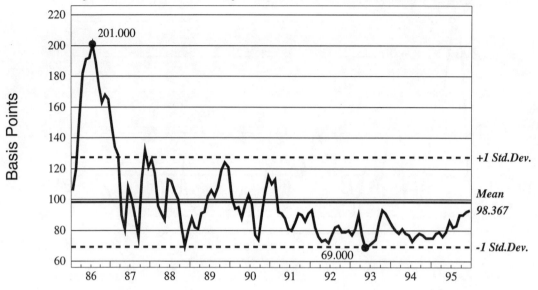

Date Range	Mean	Min.	Max.	Std.Dev.
1986-1995	98.367	69.000	201.000	28.992
1986	167.000	106.000	201.000	29.017
1987	110.000	76.000	147.000	23.085
1988	98.250	70.000	126.000	16.939
1989	101.333	81.000	124.000	14.889
1990	94.750	74.000	115.000	11.435
1991	91.500	80.000	113.000	10.158
1992	79.167	72.000	93.000	5.670
1993	80.500	69.000	93.000	8.533
1994	77.583	73.000	83.000	2.778
1995	83.583	75.000	93.000	6.431

The basic characteristics of corporate bonds are similar to those of U.S. Treasury bonds: fixed face values, interest paid semi-annually, and standard denominations of $1,000. Corporate bonds are sold to yield at a spread over Treasuries, which is determined by factors such as tenor, credit risk of the issuer, the current and anticipated supply of new issues, expectations for interest rates and the economy, and the presence of embedded options. Similar factors affect secondary market spreads, as well as the expected remaining life of the issue. Spreads may diverge for bonds with embedded options, as the securities may trade at yields that reflect the expectation that the issue will be called or refunded before maturity. The bonds comprising our data set are rated "Aa" by Moody's and have an average remaining life of 29 years. A time series of spread levels and changes for similarly-rated bonds with shorter remaining lives would behave differently over time. The "Aa" (Moody's) or "AA" (Standard & Poor's) ratings represent high-quality bonds with a great potential to meet all interest and principal payments, but with margins of protection below those of "Aaa"-rated instruments.

Corporate Bond Spreads: Industrials A

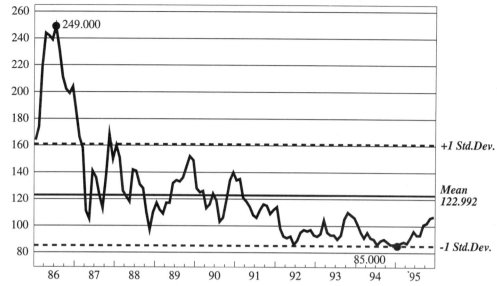

Date Range	Mean	Min.	Max.	Std.Dev.
1986-1995	122.992	85.000	249.000	37.879
1986	214.833	164.000	249.000	27.663
1987	141.000	105.000	184.000	25.078
1988	128.000	97.000	160.000	18.281
1989	129.333	109.000	152.000	14.687
1990	121.167	103.000	140.000	10.752
1991	116.667	106.000	135.000	9.335
1992	95.000	86.000	114.000	6.967
1993	98.583	90.000	110.000	7.317
1994	90.667	86.000	101.000	4.479
1995	94.667	85.000	107.000	7.691

The basic characteristics of corporate bonds are similar to those of U.S. Treasury bonds: fixed face values, interest paid semi-annually, and standard denominations of $1,000. Corporate bonds are sold to yield at a spread over Treasuries, which is determined by factors such as tenor, credit risk of the issuer, the current and anticipated supply of new issues, expectations for interest rates and the economy, and the presence of embedded options. Similar factors affect secondary market spreads, as well as the expected remaining life of the issue. Spreads may diverge for bonds with embedded options, as the securities may trade at yields that reflect the expectation that the issue will be called or refunded before maturity. The bonds comprising our data set are rated "A" by Moody's and have an average remaining life of 28 years. A time series of spread levels and changes for similarly-rated bonds with shorter remaining lives would behave differently over time. The "A" (Moody's and Standard & Poor's) ratings represent upper-medium-quality bonds with adequate principal and interest payment protection, but with higher levels of cash flow and business risk leading to an increased potential of debt service impairment versus higher-rated instruments.

Corporate Bond Spreads: Industrials BBB-Baa

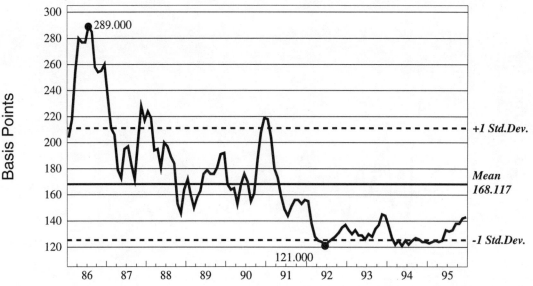

Date Range	Mean	Min.	Max.	Std.Dev.
1986-1995	168.117	121.000	289.000	42.850
1986	259.250	204.000	289.000	26.004
1987	199.583	172.000	233.000	20.438
1988	187.167	146.000	224.000	23.721
1989	172.833	150.000	192.000	12.918
1990	174.583	153.000	219.000	20.487
1991	166.583	144.000	218.000	23.169
1992	131.000	121.000	155.000	9.313
1993	133.167	126.000	145.000	6.073
1994	125.333	121.000	136.000	3.869
1995	131.667	123.000	143.000	7.390

The basic characteristics of corporate bonds are similar to those of U.S. Treasury bonds: fixed face values, interest paid semi-annually, and standard denominations of $1,000. Corporate bonds are sold to yield at a spread over Treasuries, which is determined by factors such as tenor, credit risk of the issuer, the current and anticipated supply of new issues, expectations for interest rates and the economy, and the presence of embedded options. Similar factors affect secondary market spreads, as well as the expected remaining life of the issue. Spreads may diverge for bonds with embedded options, as the securities may trade at yields that reflect the expectation that the issue will be called or refunded before maturity. The bonds comprising our data set are rated "Baa" by Moody's and have an average remaining life of 26 years. A time series of spread levels and changes for similarly-rated bonds with shorter remaining lives would behave differently over time. The "Baa" (Moody's) or "BBB" (Standard & Poor's) ratings represent only satisfactory capacity for the issuer to meet all interest and principal payments due to the absence or inconsistency of certain protective elements. This is the lowest "investment-grade" rating.

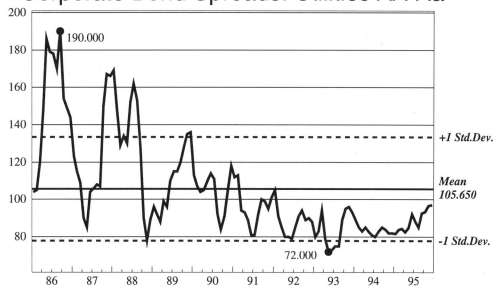

Date Range	Mean	Min.	Max.	Std.Dev.
1986-1995	105.650	72.000	190.000	27.698
1986	152.250	104.000	190.000	30.088
1987	119.167	85.000	167.000	27.405
1988	130.167	78.000	169.000	29.981
1989	110.833	88.000	136.000	16.754
1990	104.500	84.000	118.000	10.370
1991	95.833	81.000	113.000	10.107
1992	88.083	79.000	105.000	7.229
1993	83.667	72.000	96.000	9.238
1994	83.483	80.000	89.000	2.359
1995	88.517	81.700	97.100	5.535

The basic characteristics of corporate bonds are similar to those of U.S. Treasury bonds: fixed face values, interest paid semi-annually, and standard denominations of $1,000. Corporate bonds are sold to yield at a spread over Treasuries, which is determined by factors such as tenor, credit risk of the issuer, the current and anticipated supply of new issues, expectations for interest rates and the economy, and the presence of embedded options. Similar factors affect secondary market spreads, as well as the expected remaining life of the issue. Spreads may diverge for bonds with embedded options, as the securities may trade at yields that reflect the expectation that the issue will be called or refunded before maturity. The bonds comprising our data set are rated "Aa" by Moody's and have an average remaining life of 31 years. A time series of spread levels and changes for similarly-rated bonds with shorter remaining lives would behave differently over time. The "Aa" (Moody's) or "AA" (Standard & Poor's) ratings represent high-quality bonds with a great potential to meet all interest and principal payments, but with margins of protection below those of "Aaa"-rated instruments.

SPREADS ANALYSIS

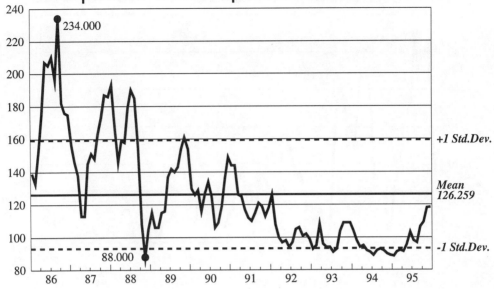

Date Range	Mean	Min.	Max.	Std.Dev.
1986-1995	126.259	88.000	234.000	33.067
1986	182.000	133.000	234.000	30.335
1987	151.583	113.000	187.000	23.926
1988	152.750	88.000	193.000	35.074
1989	132.417	106.000	161.000	19.778
1990	125.500	106.000	149.000	11.890
1991	122.000	110.000	144.000	11.354
1992	102.750	94.000	126.000	8.390
1993	99.583	91.000	109.000	7.465
1994	93.250	89.000	104.000	4.245
1995	100.758	88.600	118.400	10.339

The basic characteristics of corporate bonds are similar to those of U.S. Treasury bonds: fixed face values, interest paid semi-annually, and standard denominations of $1,000. Corporate bonds are sold to yield at a spread over Treasuries, which is determined by factors such as tenor, credit risk of the issuer, the current and anticipated supply of new issues, expectations for interest rates and the economy, and the presence of embedded options. Similar factors affect secondary market spreads, as well as the expected remaining life of the issue. Spreads may diverge for bonds with embedded options, as the securities may trade at yields that reflect the expectation that the issue will be called or refunded before maturity. The bonds comprising our data set are rated "A" by Moody's and have an average remaining life of 29 years. A time series of spread levels and changes for similarly-rated bonds with shorter remaining lives would behave differently over time. The "A" (Moody's and Standard & Poor's) ratings represent upper-medium-quality bonds with adequate principal and interest payment protection, but a higher potential of debt service impairment versus higher-rated instruments.

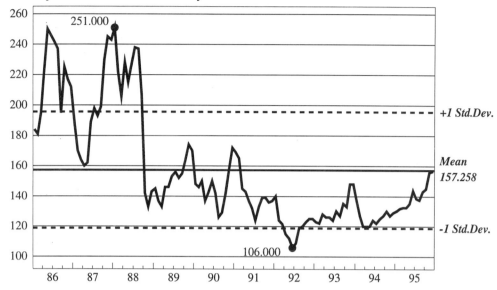

Date Range	Mean	Min.	Max.	Std.Dev.
1986-1995	157.258	106.000	251.000	38.405
1986	217.333	181.000	250.000	24.205
1987	195.083	160.000	245.000	30.216
1988	204.083	133.000	251.000	41.146
1989	152.583	133.000	174.000	12.362
1990	145.250	126.000	172.000	12.285
1991	141.583	124.000	169.000	13.056
1992	119.958	106.000	140.000	8.966
1993	130.833	122.000	148.000	8.881
1994	125.667	120.000	137.000	5.015
1995	140.200	130.300	156.800	8.999

The basic characteristics of corporate bonds are similar to those of U.S. Treasury bonds: fixed face values, interest paid semi-annually, and standard denominations of $1,000. Corporate bonds are sold to yield at a spread over Treasuries, which is determined by factors such as tenor, credit risk of the issuer, the current and anticipated supply of new issues, expectations for interest rates and the economy, and the presence of embedded options. Similar factors affect secondary market spreads, as well as the expected remaining life of the issue. Spreads may diverge for bonds with embedded options, as the securities may trade at yields that reflect the expectation that the issue will be called or refunded before maturity. The bonds comprising our data set are rated "Baa" by Moody's and have an average remaining life of 28 years. A time series of spread levels and changes for similarly-rated bonds with shorter remaining lives would behave differently over time. The "Baa" (Moody's) or "BBB" (Standard & Poor's) ratings represent only satisfactory capacity for the issuer to meet all interest and principal payments due to the absence or inconsistency of certain protective elements. This is the lowest "investment-grade" rating.

PART 1
Spreads Analysis

SECTION VI
Economic Indicators

Federal Funds Rate

Included with the chart of each economic indicator that follows is a graph of the Federal Funds rate. This is the rate that banks charge for lending each other funds overnight. The markets use this key rate as a barometer of the stance of monetary policy. In fact, the Federal Reserve establishes a target for the Federal Funds rate. If this target is raised, the Fed is thought to have tightened monetary policy, that is, to have made policy more restrictive. In contrast, if this target is lowered, the Fed has eased monetary policy, or made it less restrictive.

The Federal Reserve looks at a whole host of economic indicators, including many of those that follow, in determining its monetary policy stance. Moreover, while it takes a little while for a change in monetary policy to be felt by the economy, these indicators will ultimately reflect a change in monetary conditions as well. By juxtaposing the behavior of the Federal Funds rate on to the history of these economic indicators, the reader can see how the economy was functioning just prior to changes in monetary policy, and also how it subsequently responded to these changes.

Chain-weighted Real GDP

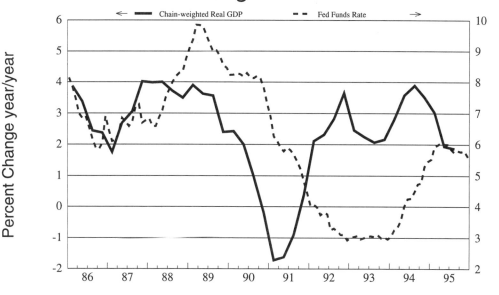

Date Range	Mean	Min.	Max.	Std.Dev.
1986-1995	2.412	-1.726	4.024	1.496
1986	3.016	2.373	3.879	0.737
1987	2.884	1.757	4.024	0.938
1988	3.801	3.501	4.004	0.239
1989	3.372	2.391	3.905	0.670
1990	1.298	-0.197	2.420	1.168
1991	-0.969	-1.726	0.385	0.973
1992	2.721	2.107	3.651	0.689
1993	2.232	2.068	2.457	0.166
1994	3.452	2.807	3.898	0.461
*1995	2.278	1.863	3.029	0.651

*Data not available for the full year due to delays caused by the government shutdown.

This year the Commerce Department is switching the way in which it calculates real GDP. For nearly 50 years, real GDP has been calculated using fixed weights. To remove the impact of inflation, the goods and services produced each year have been evaluated in the prices of a common base year--currently 1987. That is, real GDP in any year indicates how much the economy produced if the prices of goods and services were the same as in 1987. As the economy moves away from the base year, a problem arises with the old method of calculating real GDP -- substitution bias. Specifically, as prices change, people and businesses change their purchases, substituting away from goods whose prices are rising relative to others and substituting toward goods whose prices are falling relative to others. Consequently, output increases most for those goods with declining relative prices. Evaluating the current production of these goods at their previous relatively higher prices tends to overstate real GDP growth. For example, a $2,000 computer purchased in 1995 would have cost $6,000 in 1987--three times as much. So, each $1 spent on computers in 1995 counts as $3 of real spending. This means that the weight given to computers in the calculation of real GDP has tripled over the past eight years. The chain-weighting procedure minimizes this "substitution bias" by using prices close to the year in question. Moving through time forms a chain of weights that gives this approach its name.

SPREADS ANALYSIS

Nominal GDP: Gross Domestic Product

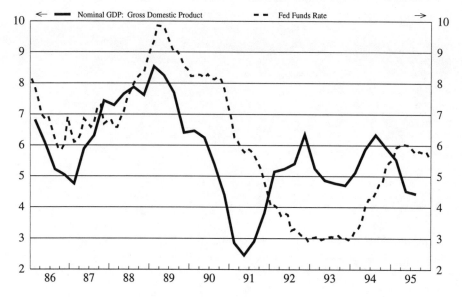

Date Range	Mean	Min.	Max.	Std.Dev.
1986-1995	5.715	2.457	8.541	1.455
1986	5.790	5.048	6.811	0.816
1987	6.097	4.759	7.438	1.107
1988	7.611	7.291	7.875	0.241
1989	7.723	6.398	8.541	0.950
1990	5.622	4.399	6.461	0.938
1991	3.008	2.457	3.819	0.576
1992	5.535	5.148	6.343	0.549
1993	4.900	4.711	5.244	0.238
1994	5.814	5.122	6.335	0.506
*1995	4.831	4.431	5.537	0.613

*Data not available for the full year due to delays caused by the government shutdown.

Gross Domestic Product (GDP) is the broadest measure of aggregate economic activity. It is the market value of all goods and services produced within a country during the year. GDP is typically calculated from the spending on goods and services by the four major spending groups within the economy--households, businesses, governments, and foreigners. While GDP is most often presented and analyzed after having been adjusted for the effects of inflation, it is also report in nominal dollars; that is, the value of goods and services produced is evaluated at current market prices.

National Purchasing Managers' Index

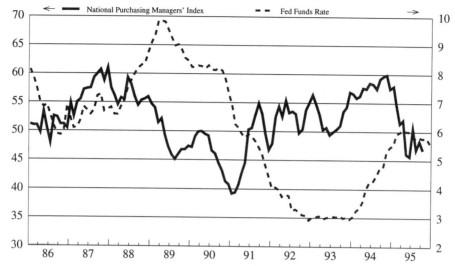

Source: Datastream

Date Range	Mean	Min.	Max.	Std.Dev.
1986-1995	52.061	39.200	61.000	4.917
1986	51.058	48.000	53.400	1.400
1987	57.492	52.600	61.000	2.607
1988	56.217	54.500	59.300	1.429
1989	48.925	45.100	54.700	3.357
1990	46.450	40.800	50.000	3.329
1991	47.058	39.200	54.900	5.614
1992	52.642	47.900	55.400	2.239
1993	52.550	49.400	56.900	2.619
1994	57.867	55.900	59.900	1.300
1995	50.010	45.700	57.900	4.018

The National Association of Purchasing Managers' index is a key indicator of the health of the manufacturing sector. The headline index is actually a weighted average of five diffusion indexes. Each of the five diffusion indexes is calculated from the answers to questions by the purchasing executives of about 300 industrial companies, spanning all 50 states and 20 different manufacturing sectors. The questions cover orders, production, employment, vendor performance, and inventories. For each question there are only three possible answers--higher, lower, or the same relative to the previous month. For example, each purchasing manager will convey whether production this month was higher, lower, or the same as last month. Each individual diffusion index within the overall index is calculated by adding the percentage of positive responses to one-half of those who reported conditions unchanged. This index is centered around 50 and ranges from 0 to 100. Readings above 50 generally indicate an expanding manufacturing sector, while readings below 50 generally imply a manufacturing sector in decline. A reading of zero would indicate that every respondent reported a decline, while a reading of 100 would indicate that every respondent reported an increase.

Employment (Total Non-farm Payrolls)

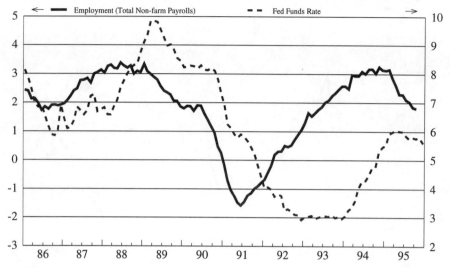

Source: Datastream

Date Range	Mean	Min.	Max.	Std.Dev.
1986-1995	1.831	-1.579	3.385	1.319
1986	2.011	1.740	2.442	0.227
1987	2.623	1.972	3.138	0.384
1988	3.192	3.001	3.385	0.122
1989	2.559	1.867	3.333	0.462
1990	1.418	0.259	1.905	0.578
1991	-1.059	-1.579	-0.169	0.392
1992	0.310	-0.672	1.067	0.519
1993	1.959	1.309	2.581	0.398
1994	2.981	2.492	3.249	0.232
1995	2.409	1.800	3.151	0.498

Payroll employment figures are one of myriad statistics included in the Labor Department's monthly employment report. They are simply a tally of the number of people being paid as employees by nonfarm business establishments and governmental units. The monthly figures reported are the changes in total nonfarm payroll employment. These figures are compiled from surveys of over 300,000 establishments that employ workers. Since income is an important determinant of consumption, and most income is generated by employment, the employment figures are widely followed as one of the most important indicators of economic activity. The widely followed civilian unemployment rate is not calculated from the same survey as are the nonfarm payroll figures. Rather, this rate is calculated from a survey of nearly 60,000 households. While the trends depicted by these two surveys are extremely similar, the monthly results from the household survey are more volatile than those from the establishment survey. Consequently, the financial markets generally pay more attention to the month-to-month figures from the establishment survey.

Retail Sales

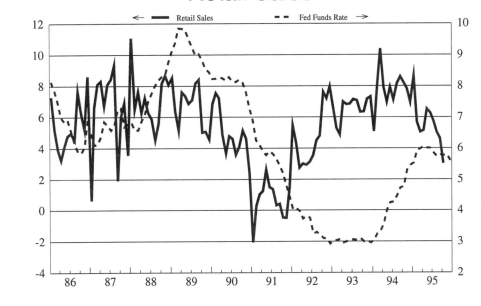

Date Range	Mean	Min.	Max.	Std.Dev.
1986-1995	5.577	-2.053	11.075	2.486
1986	5.474	3.244	8.612	1.638
1987	6.221	0.627	9.343	2.763
1988	7.161	4.535	11.075	1.725
1989	6.684	4.573	8.523	1.431
1990	4.952	2.432	7.555	1.553
1991	0.600	-2.053	2.614	1.218
1992	4.771	2.745	7.967	1.906
1993	6.577	4.867	7.317	0.769
1994	7.766	5.077	10.382	1.238
1995	5.567	3.020	8.624	1.450

Retail sales are a measure of the dollar value (not adjusted for inflation) of the merchandise sold at retail stores. Sales data are for all businesses classified as retail trade according to the Standard Industrial Classification. Sales are net after deductions for refunds and allowances for merchandise returned by customers. These figures are a major barometer of consumer spending trends because they account for nearly 1/2 of total consumer spending. Retail sales are broadly broken into two categories: durable and nondurable goods. Durable goods, those expected to last three years or more, generally account for about 35% of total sales, while nondurables account for the rest. Sales at automobile dealerships are an extremely important component of retail sales, accounting for about 60% of sales of durable goods and more than 20% of total retail sales. Swings in auto sales typically dominate the durable goods component and at times total retail sales.

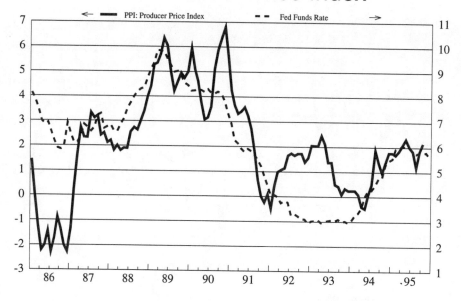

PPI: Producer Price Index

Date Range	Mean	Min.	Max.	Std.Dev.
1986-1995	2.048	-2.292	6.794	2.079
1986	-1.326	-2.292	1.442	1.099
1987	2.060	-1.327	3.324	1.340
1988	2.496	1.808	3.970	0.694
1989	5.134	4.228	6.343	0.643
1990	4.923	3.070	6.794	1.270
1991	2.201	-0.245	4.248	1.654
1992	1.213	-0.489	1.734	0.670
1993	1.248	0.081	2.445	0.886
1994	0.631	-0.477	1.856	0.810
1995	1.867	1.189	2.318	0.309

The Producer Price Index (PPI) is a weighted-average measure of the prices of a fixed basket of over 3,450 goods purchased in primary markets by producers. The PPI is a measure solely of commodities prices; there are no prices of services included. Producer price information is obtained at three levels of production--finished goods, intermediate components, and crude materials. Prices are sampled monthly and, in most cases, information is collected in the week that contains the 13th of the month. The PPI for finished goods is a major indicator of commodity price pressures because it accounts for price changes all across the manufacturing sector. One should hesitate in using information on producer prices to anticipate price increases at the consumer level, however. Although the general trends should exhibit common similarities, the month-to-month behavior can be quite dissimilar.

SPREADS ANALYSIS

CPI: Consumer Price Index

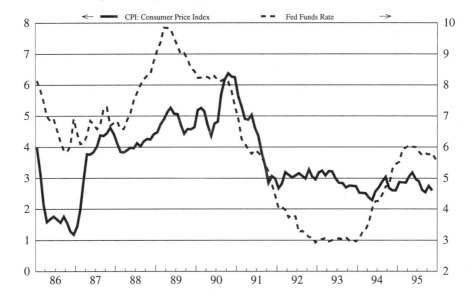

Date Range	Mean	Min.	Max.	Std.Dev.
1986-1995	3.564	1.187	6.375	1.171
1986	1.950	1.187	3.974	0.818
1987	3.668	1.456	4.620	1.020
1988	4.073	3.829	4.408	0.181
1989	4.796	4.431	5.272	0.279
1990	5.417	4.362	6.375	0.710
1991	4.235	2.846	5.642	0.980
1992	3.033	2.671	3.277	0.163
1993	2.963	2.691	3.244	0.218
1994	2.605	2.287	3.034	0.207
1995	2.836	2.544	3.184	0.197

The Consumer Price Index (CPI) is a weighted-average measure of the price of a fixed market basket of goods and services purchased by consumers. The basket contains more than 350 goods and services, of which approximately 55% are services and the remaining 45% are goods. Households are surveyed periodically to determine the spending patterns used to construct the weights of the consumer basket.

There are two Consumer Price Indices. The most common one (featured here) is the CPI-U, which reflects a market basket consumed by the typical urban household. However, the second CPI, CPI-W, is the one used to adjust union wage contracts and Social Security benefits for inflation. It reflects a market basket consumed by wage earners only.

SPREADS ANALYSIS

Industrial Production

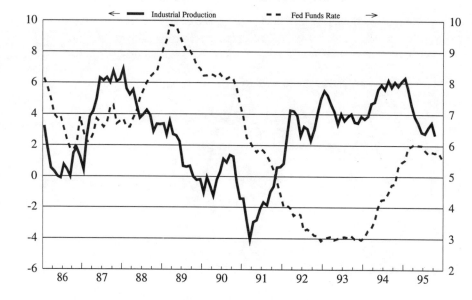

Date Range	Mean	Min.	Max.	Std.Dev.
1986-1995	2.664	-4.064	6.891	2.544
1986	0.957	-0.106	3.222	0.992
1987	4.983	0.424	6.749	1.924
1988	4.452	2.883	6.891	1.170
1989	1.557	-0.229	3.550	1.436
1990	-0.003	-1.435	1.366	0.998
1991	-1.681	-4.064	0.624	1.418
1992	3.263	0.842	4.998	1.117
1993	4.100	3.370	5.501	0.689
1994	5.338	3.700	6.181	0.862
1995	3.875	2.678	6.324	1.251

Industrial production is a fixed-weight measure of the physical output of the nation's factories, mines, and utilities. It does not include the production of services. Taken together, these goods-producing industry groups account for about 42% of the economy (as measured by real GDP). In contrast to most of the other indicators, industrial production is not compiled by the federal government. Rather, it is produced by the Federal Reserve. The measure is an index based upon physical quantities of output (for example, barrels of oil, car assemblies, tons of steel, kilowatts of electricity, etc.). About 85% of the index of industrial production is manufacturing output.

Capacity Utilization

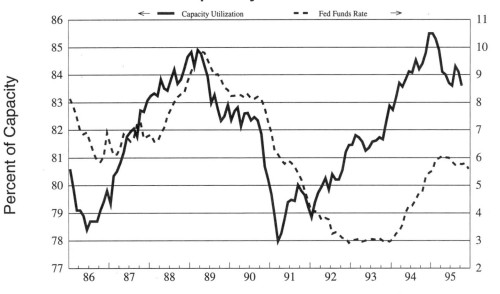

Date Range	Mean	Min.	Max.	Std.Dev.
1986-1995	81.930	77.986	85.500	1.990
1986	79.200	78.400	80.600	0.630
1987	81.513	79.342	83.072	1.104
1988	83.746	83.239	84.648	0.436
1989	83.651	82.333	84.898	0.961
1990	82.095	80.228	82.811	0.813
1991	79.214	77.986	80.015	0.623
1992	80.173	78.847	81.454	0.714
1993	81.742	81.250	82.872	0.439
1994	84.051	82.730	85.500	0.736
1995	84.310	83.600	85.500	0.692

A companion to the index of industrial production is the rate of capacity utilization, which provides a measure of the degree of slack in the industrial sector. This measure is simply the level of output divided by the level of capacity. While the index of industrial production provides the measure of output, capacity must be estimated. The Fed defines capacity as the maximum level of production that can be obtained using normal employee work schedules with existing equipment (allowing for normal downtime due to maintenance and repair). Capacity measures are generated from yearly surveys. However, since survey information is obtained so infrequently, the Fed assumes that capacity grows at its trend rate and then makes adjustments after surveys have been conducted. Consequently, the rate of capacity utilization is subject to substantial revisions. Despite its shortcomings, the rate of capacity utilization is a useful indicator for gauging inflation pressures. When little excess capacity exists (particularly, when the utilization rate is 85% or higher), inflation pressures have typically begun to build.

Goods and Services Trade Balance

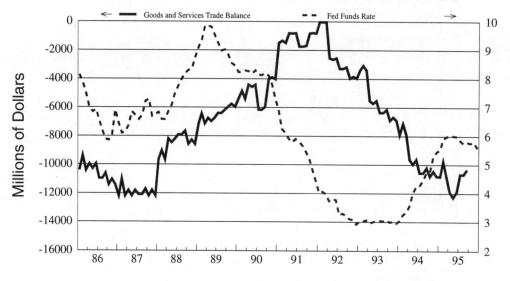

Source: Datastream

Date Range	Mean	Min.	Max.	Std.Dev.
1986-1995	-7120.453	-12279.747	-34.418	3626.707
1986	-10555.834	-11393.511	-9381.556	617.319
1987	-11936.167	-12190.835	-11009.600	348.784
1988	-8505.166	-9646.791	-7658.804	642.575
1989	-6477.500	-7122.422	-5762.283	462.864
1990	-4938.750	-6156.870	-3890.543	844.506
1991	-1190.417	-1737.011	-789.783	417.360
1992	-2449.917	-3964.630	-34.418	1537.311
1993	-5486.833	-6892.109	-3068.178	1408.737
1994	-9623.833	-10795.413	-7124.444	1276.101
*1995	-11013.333	-12279.747	-9769.200	825.172

*Data not available for the full year due to delays caused by the government shutdown.

The goods and services trade balance is the value of the difference between a country's exports and its imports of goods and services. Historically, the U.S. has run a trade deficit, meaning that the U.S. has imported more from abroad than it has exported. U.S. exports reflect, among other things, the strength of demand abroad and the competitiveness of the U.S. dollar in the foreign exchange market. Similarly, U.S. imports reflect the strength of U.S. demand. In terms of U.S. GDP, exports add to U.S. output; imports subtract from U.S. output, as they indicate the portion of U.S. demand that is satisfied by production abroad.

Housing Starts: Total New Private Housing

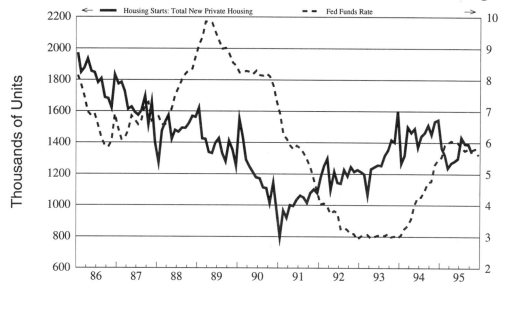

Date Range	Mean	Min.	Max.	Std.Dev.
1986-1995	1380.822	798.000	1972.000	241.994
1986	1811.917	1623.000	1972.000	103.790
1987	1630.500	1400.000	1784.000	108.668
1988	1487.833	1271.000	1573.000	82.510
1989	1382.083	1251.000	1621.000	95.005
1990	1203.167	969.000	1551.000	164.399
1991	1008.750	798.000	1103.000	84.396
1992	1201.417	1099.000	1297.000	55.051
1993	1296.333	1068.000	1602.000	135.333
1994	1445.917	1266.000	1545.000	86.331
*1995	1332.200	1238.000	1432.000	62.057

*Data not available for the full year due to delays caused by the government shutdown.

Housing starts are a measure of the number of residential units on which construction is begun each month. A housing unit is considered started when excavation of the building site commences. Housing starts include nearly all types of accommodation designed as family living quarters. However, housing provided by conversion of nonresidential space and the production of mobile homes are not included in the calculation of housing starts. Data are available by major geographic region--Northeast, Midwest, South, and West--and by number of units per structure--single-family homes vs. multifamily units. Information on housing starts are an extremely useful economic indicator, as they often turn up or down ahead of the rest of the economy. Most turning points in the postwar business cycle have been preceded by changes in the behavior of housing starts.

SPREADS ANALYSIS

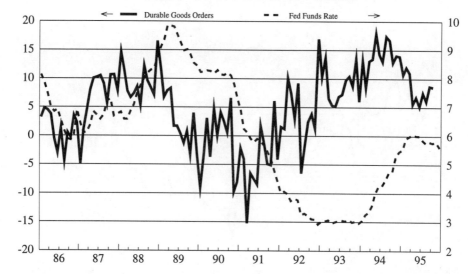

Source: Datastream

Date Range	Mean	Min.	Max.	Std.Dev.
1986-1995	5.007	-15.227	17.849	6.703
1986	1.339	-4.380	4.836	2.952
1987	6.973	-4.907	10.667	4.764
1988	9.674	5.407	16.588	3.398
1989	2.943	-3.430	11.702	4.834
1990	-1.001	-9.784	6.611	5.674
1991	-4.279	-15.227	6.128	5.323
1992	4.088	-6.470	16.948	6.116
1993	8.639	5.195	13.656	2.928
1994	14.026	8.436	17.849	2.503
*1995	8.194	5.171	11.966	2.401

*Data not available for the full year due to delays caused by the government shutdown.

Durable goods orders are a measure of the new orders placed with domestic manufacturers for immediate and future delivery of factory goods. A durable good is one with an expected life of three years or more. A new order is accompanied by a legally binding agreement to purchase the good at a future date. Durable goods orders are measured at market prices and hence include the effects of inflation. The report of durable goods orders also contains information on unfilled orders (that is, order backlogs), and shipments (that is, sales). These figures provide a comprehensive look at the manufacturing sector and often are a useful indicator of the pace of demand growth. However, month-to-month changes are characteristically quite volatile, being swung by the "bunching" of orders for "big-ticket" items, such as aircraft and military equipment.

Personal Income

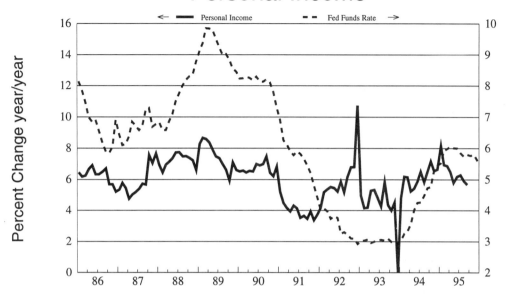

Date Range	Mean	Min.	Max.	Std.Dev.
1986-1995	6.029	0.032	10.745	1.396
1986	6.239	5.217	6.906	0.488
1987	5.883	4.764	7.653	0.980
1988	7.205	6.452	7.750	0.409
1989	7.484	5.920	8.650	0.883
1990	6.700	6.205	7.478	0.345
1991	3.996	3.380	5.223	0.518
1992	6.035	4.161	10.745	1.653
1993	4.313	0.032	5.829	1.461
1994	6.069	4.810	7.155	0.669
*1995	6.474	5.676	8.146	0.767

*Data not available for the full year due to delays caused by the government shutdown.

Personal income is the fuel for consumption. It is composed of several components; the largest component is wages and salaries, which comprises about 60% of the total. Income also includes proprietors' income, income from rents, dividends and interest, and transfer payments. Given the many types of personal income, the source data are quite varied. For example, wage and salary estimates come largely from the payroll employment data collected by the Labor Department. Data on transfer payments come from the Social Security Administration, the Veterans Administration, and the Treasury. Dividend income is estimated from a sample of corporate dividend payments. And interest income data is derived from household asset information collected by the Federal Reserve.

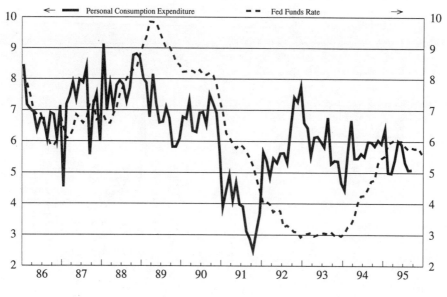

Date Range	Mean	Min.	Max.	Std.Dev.
1986-1995	6.259	2.495	9.136	1.322
1986	6.874	6.062	8.461	0.626
1987	7.080	4.532	8.382	1.134
1988	7.989	6.993	9.136	0.714
1989	6.901	5.823	8.151	0.804
1990	6.760	5.695	7.496	0.493
1991	3.766	2.495	4.915	0.740
1992	6.000	4.849	7.752	0.963
1993	5.842	4.675	6.769	0.616
1994	5.714	4.436	6.675	0.527
*1995	5.463	4.980	6.388	0.513

*Data not available for the full year due to delays caused by the government shutdown.

Consumers comprise the largest share of GDP, accounting for nearly two-thirds of GDP. Consequently, information on personal consumption expenditure (PCE) is crucial in gauging the state of the economy. The consumer spending data in this release are more comprehensive than the retail sales figures--which measure only the spending on goods. In contrast, personal consumption expenditures cover spending by individuals and households on both goods and services. They are broken down into three categories: spending on durable goods, nondurable goods, and services. Spending on durable goods comprises almost 13% of total consumption; spending on nondurables is about 30% of the total, while services consumption is by far the largest component--comprising about 57%. Spending on durable and nondurable goods are the most volatile components of total PCE. They account for most of the cyclical variability.

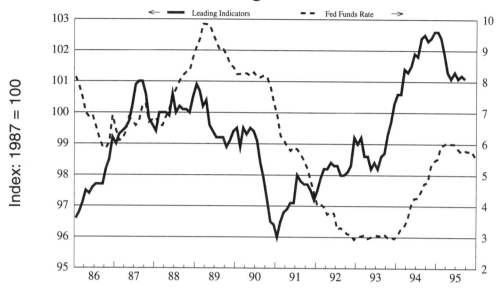

Date Range	Mean	Min.	Max.	Std.Dev.
1986-1995	99.294	96.000	102.600	1.595
1986	97.667	96.600	99.200	0.716
1987	100.000	99.000	101.000	0.714
1988	100.067	99.400	100.600	0.299
1989	99.683	98.900	100.900	0.682
1990	98.467	96.400	99.500	1.184
1991	97.192	96.000	98.000	0.587
1992	98.200	97.500	99.200	0.398
1993	98.900	98.200	100.300	0.632
1994	101.775	100.600	102.600	0.706
*1995	101.556	101.100	102.600	0.592

*Data not available for the full year due to delays caused by the government shutdown.

The index of leading indicators is a collection of eleven different economic variables, each of which is itself thought to be a leading indicator of the pace of economic activity. The overall index is designed to give advance warning of turning points in the business cycle. The eleven components are: the average manufacturing workweek, initial unemployment insurance claims, new orders for consumer goods, vendor performance (that is, the speed of deliveries), orders for plant and equipment, building permits, change in unfilled durable goods orders, change in sensitive materials (that is, commodities) prices, consumer expectations, M2 money supply (adjusted for inflation), and the S&P 500 equity price index. The index of leading indicators has typically turned down nearly a year prior to the beginning of an economic recession. However, it has tended to overpredict business cycle downturns; that is, predict recessions that do not materialize. Since the components are generally known in advance of the monthly release of the overall index, financial markets rarely react to the index's actual release.

SPREADS ANALYSIS

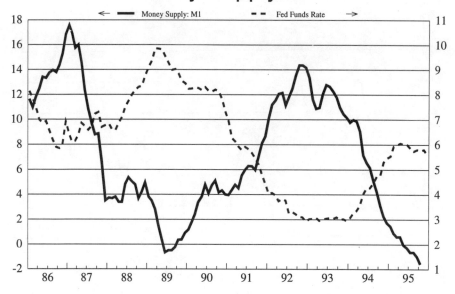

Date Range	Mean	Min.	Max.	Std.Dev.
1986-1995	7.152	-1.594	17.587	5.090
1986	13.478	10.991	16.858	1.633
1987	11.790	3.506	17.587	4.465
1988	4.230	3.375	5.358	0.711
1989	0.980	-0.668	3.803	1.583
1990	3.644	1.183	5.118	1.237
1991	5.950	3.948	8.645	1.463
1992	12.406	10.088	14.359	1.401
1993	11.662	10.172	13.372	0.996
1994	6.244	1.719	9.983	3.018
1995	-0.060	-1.594	1.457	0.944

The M1 money supply is comprised of the most liquid liabilities of the banking system and the Federal Reserve. It includes currency in circulation, demand deposits at commercial banks, other checkable deposits at depository institutions, and travelers checks. M1 was once a monetary aggregate for which the Federal Reserve established an annual target range. However, the financial deregulation and innovation of the early 1980s compromised the value of targeting M1, at least to the Fed, and since 1986 the Fed has no longer established a target range for this aggregate. However, there remains a small body of market analysts who continue to look at the behavior of M1 as an indicator of the stance of monetary policy.

SPREADS ANALYSIS

Money Supply: M2

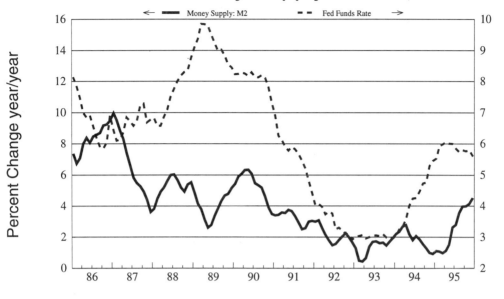

Date Range	Mean	Min.	Max.	Std.Dev.
1986-1995	4.066	0.436	9.973	2.370
1986	8.271	6.730	9.479	0.871
1987	6.685	3.617	9.973	2.103
1988	5.228	3.812	6.034	0.634
1989	3.955	2.610	5.173	0.847
1990	5.337	3.478	6.325	0.924
1991	3.230	2.509	3.745	0.416
1992	2.113	1.475	3.083	0.530
1993	1.335	0.436	1.943	0.522
1994	1.887	0.929	2.777	0.607
1995	2.614	0.970	4.526	1.395

The M2 monetary aggregate is comprised of a broader range of liabilities of the banking system than is M1. It includes the liabilities in M1 plus savings accounts, time deposits of less than $100,000, money market deposit accounts, general-purpose money market mutual funds, overnight repurchase agreements, and overnight Eurodollar deposits of U.S. residents at foreign branches of U.S. banks. Changes in M2 money supply are widely followed as indicators of the thrust of monetary policy. For example, an acceleration in the growth rate of M2 is typically seen as indicating a more accommodative monetary policy. However, over the past several years, the relationship between economic activity and M2 has deteriorated. Portfolio shifts have generated wide swings in M2 without any associated change in the pace of economic activity. Consequently, while the Fed still maintains a target range for M2, it has reduced the emphasis it places on M2 as a guide to the conduct of monetary policy

PART 2
Foreign Interest Rates

SECTION I
Germany

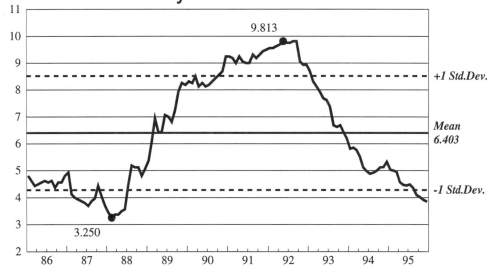

Date Range	Mean	Min.	Max.	Std.Dev.
1986-1995	6.403	3.250	9.813	2.116
1986	4.589	4.375	4.813	0.129
1987	4.034	3.688	4.938	0.349
1988	4.188	3.250	5.188	0.831
1989	6.979	5.375	8.250	0.858
1990	8.417	8.125	9.250	0.316
1991	9.208	9.000	9.500	0.169
1992	9.526	8.938	9.813	0.343
1993	7.365	6.188	8.688	0.822
1994	5.288	4.890	5.847	0.359
1995	4.439	3.857	5.031	0.412

Eurocurrency deposits/loans are bank liabilities/assets denominated in a foreign currency. The location of the bank accepting the deposit or making the loan is the determining factor. Deutsche Mark-denominated deposits in London, for example, are Euro-Deutsche Marks even if the depositor is a German citizen and the bank is a London branch of a German bank. These deposits have the same terms as those available for deposits denominated in the domestic currency; that is, funds may be placed for as short as overnight or as long as 12 months. The interest rate obtained depends on market demand and supply and fluctuates daily. Rates are influenced primarily by the conditions prevailing in the respective domestic markets, the most important of which is the current stance of domestic monetary policy, and, to a lesser extent, by conditions in the foreign exchange markets. London is by far the largest market for Eurocurrency-denominated deposits and loans. The interest rate quoted for deposits, the London interbank offered rate (LIBOR), is frequently used as the benchmark short-term interest rate.

The Euro-Deutsche Mark market is the world's second largest Euromarket behind the Euro-dollar. Its position is based on: (1) the DM being the most important reserve currency behind the U.S. Dollar, (2) the key role played by the DM in the exchange rate mechanism of the European Monetary System, and (3) the relatively arduous reserve requirements placed on deposits held in German banks.

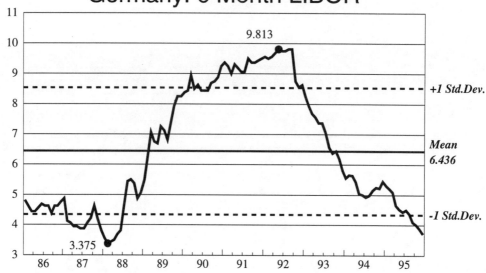

Germany: 6 Month LIBOR

Source: Datastream

Date Range	Mean	Min.	Max.	Std.Dev.
1986-1995	6.436	3.375	9.813	2.095
1986	4.599	4.375	4.813	0.129
1987	4.133	3.813	4.875	0.320
1988	4.354	3.375	5.500	0.867
1989	7.104	5.500	8.250	0.804
1990	8.646	8.375	9.250	0.267
1991	9.286	9.000	9.500	0.174
1992	9.432	8.563	9.813	0.487
1993	7.052	5.813	8.250	0.766
1994	5.275	4.932	5.656	0.263
1995	4.481	3.711	5.296	0.516

Eurocurrency deposits/loans are bank liabilities/assets denominated in a foreign currency. The location of the bank accepting the deposit or making the loan is the determining factor. Deutsche Mark-denominated deposits in London, for example, are Euro-Deutsche Marks even if the depositor is a German citizen and the bank is a London branch of a German bank. These deposits have the same terms as those available for deposits denominated in the domestic currency; that is, funds may be placed for as short as overnight or as long as for 12 months. The interest rate obtained depends on market demand and supply and fluctuates daily. Rates are influenced primarily by the conditions prevailing in the respective domestic markets, the most important of which is the current stance of domestic monetary policy, and, to a lesser extent, by conditions in the foreign exchange markets. London is by far the largest market for Eurocurrency-denominated deposits and loans. The interest rate quoted for deposits, the London interbank offered rate (LIBOR), is frequently used as the benchmark short-term interest rate.

The Euro-Deutsche Mark market is the world's second largest Euromarket behind the Euro-dollar. Its position is based on: (1) the DM being the most important reserve currency behind the U.S. Dollar, (2) the key role played by the DM in the exchange rate mechanism of the European Monetary System, and (3) the relatively arduous reserve requirements placed on deposits held in German banks.

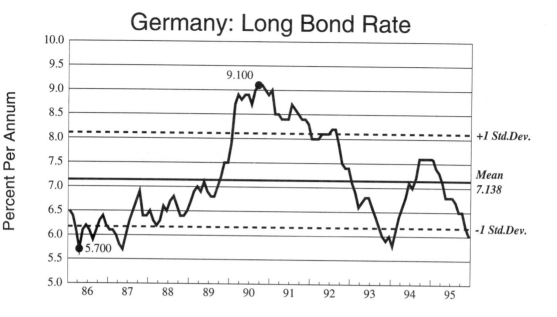

Date Range	Mean	Min.	Max.	Std.Dev.
1986-1995	7.138	5.700	9.100	0.968
1986	6.167	5.700	6.500	0.223
1987	6.242	5.700	6.900	0.358
1988	6.483	6.200	6.800	0.175
1989	7.025	6.700	7.500	0.260
1990	8.825	7.900	9.100	0.319
1991	8.508	8.300	9.000	0.188
1992	7.908	7.400	8.200	0.300
1993	6.500	5.900	7.100	0.395
1994	6.891	5.800	7.600	0.617
1995	6.808	6.000	7.600	0.480

Ten-year government bonds, called Bunds, are issued with a minimum denomination of DM1,000. They are the principal bond issued by the German government. Occasionally, the German government will issue Bunds with maturities longer than ten years, such as in 1993 when long term rates were very low. Bunds pay interest annually on a 30/360 basis. Yields are determined by market supply and demand conditions. Inflation expectations are one of the key factors behind Bund yields. Bunds are essentially free of default risk and have active secondary and futures markets.

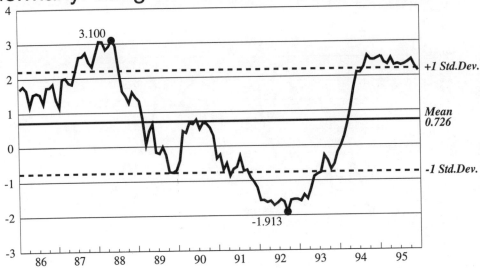

Date Range	Mean	Min.	Max.	Std.Dev.
1986-1995	0.726	-1.913	3.100	1.488
1986	1.578	1.200	1.838	0.202
1987	2.208	1.163	2.731	0.467
1988	2.296	1.275	3.100	0.758
1989	0.046	-0.750	1.325	0.660
1990	0.408	-0.412	0.775	0.392
1991	-0.700	-1.200	-0.250	0.277
1992	-1.618	-1.913	-1.538	0.106
1993	-0.865	-1.588	-0.188	0.480
1994	1.607	-0.012	2.594	0.955
1995	2.369	2.143	2.569	0.114

Financial assets are available in a range of maturities, from overnight to over 10 years. A yield curve compares yields at a given point in time across this maturity spectrum. Yields out the curve are essentially an average of what shorter-term rates are expected to be over the intervening period, say, the next 2 years, 5 years, or 10 years. So, the yield curve, whatever its shape may be at any given moment, indicates how the markets expect rates to move. And that, in turn, reveals a great deal about where the economy is headed, because expectations of what will happen to interest rates have a tremendous effect on the economy. A shorthand way to view the yield curve is by observing the behavior of the difference between the yield on a long-term security (usually a 10-year bond) and the yield on a short-term security (usually a 3-month deposit).

During an economic expansion (generally normal times), the market looks ahead and sees that continued economic growth is likely to push short rates higher than their current levels. Thus, the average of expected short rates will rise as we move further from the present. The result: long rates are higher than short rates--the yield curve is upward sloping. The opposite, a downward sloping yield curve, represents expectations that in the future short rates will be lower than they currently are. The yield curve's shape will also reflect supply/demand factors at different maturities.

The yield curve in Germany changed from inverted to normal over the course of 1994, reflecting long term rates moving up along with international bond markets, particularly in the U.S.

PART 2
Foreign Interest Rates

SECTION II
United Kingdom

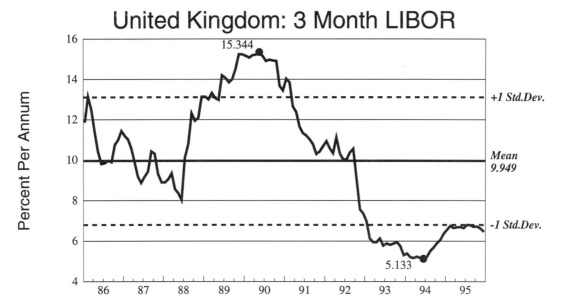

Date Range	Mean	Min.	Max.	Std.Dev.
1986-1995	9.949	5.133	15.344	3.155
1986	11.005	9.813	13.125	1.098
1987	9.865	8.875	11.188	0.824
1988	10.223	8.031	13.125	1.770
1989	13.879	12.969	15.250	0.820
1990	14.829	13.438	15.344	0.616
1991	11.697	10.297	14.031	1.266
1992	9.854	7.375	11.125	1.234
1993	5.956	5.313	7.000	0.390
1994	5.502	5.133	6.363	0.412
1995	6.675	6.468	6.801	0.093

Sterling-denominated deposits and loans in London are the counterparts to Eurocurrency deposits and loans in London. However, since these deposits and loans are denominated in the domestic currency (pounds sterling), they are not technically Eurocurrency assets/liabilities. Nonetheless, the nature of the agreements and terms available are identical to those for deposits and loans denominated in Eurocurrencies--from overnight to 12 months. Sterling London interbank offered rates (LIBOR), the rates in London on these deposits, are market-determined, but are largely reflective of the current stance of British monetary policy. Britain's financial markets are generally free of regulation (to protect London's status as one of the world's leading financial markets) and hence, sterling LIBOR behaves much as do Eurocurrency rates.

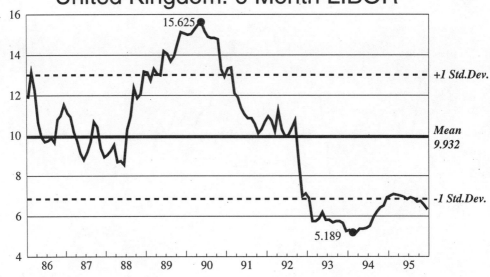

Date Range	Mean	Min.	Max.	Std.Dev.
1986-1995	9.932	5.189	15.625	3.080
1986	10.846	9.656	13.125	1.147
1987	9.854	8.813	11.125	0.804
1988	10.386	8.563	13.188	1.647
1989	13.823	12.750	15.125	0.806
1990	14.763	12.938	15.625	0.817
1991	11.387	10.125	13.375	1.090
1992	9.786	7.000	11.250	1.426
1993	5.846	5.250	6.875	0.385
1994	5.784	5.189	6.929	0.600
1995	6.847	6.327	7.105	0.229

Sterling-denominated deposits and loans in London are the counterparts to Eurocurrency deposits and loans in London. However, since these deposits and loans are denominated in the domestic currency (pounds sterling), they are not technically Eurocurrency assets/liabilities. Nonetheless, the nature of the agreements and terms available are identical to those for deposits and loans denominated in Eurocurrencies--from overnight to 12 months. Sterling London interbank offered rates (LIBOR), the rates in London on these deposits, are market-determined, but are largely reflective of the current stance of British monetary policy. Britain's financial markets are generally free of regulation (to protect London's status as one of the world's leading financial markets) and hence, sterling LIBOR behaves much as do Eurocurrency rates.

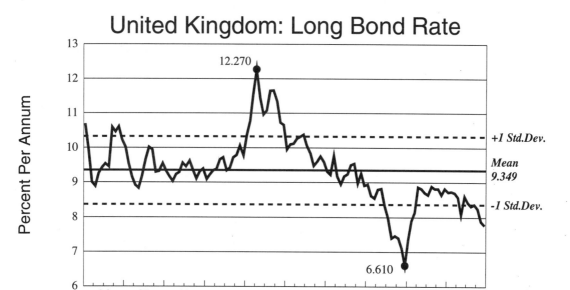

Date Range	Mean	Min.	Max.	Std.Dev.
1986-1995	9.349	6.610	12.270	0.979
1986	9.841	8.890	10.690	0.660
1987	9.457	8.840	10.020	0.406
1988	9.321	9.030	9.620	0.174
1989	9.543	9.090	10.060	0.285
1990	11.210	10.380	12.270	0.540
1991	9.957	9.480	10.380	0.302
1992	9.253	8.910	9.770	0.255
1993	8.002	6.610	8.940	0.783
1994	8.537	7.350	8.890	0.485
1995	8.369	7.770	8.740	0.327

The UK government bonds are called Gilts. Gilts pay interest semi-annually on an actual/365-day year basis. Yields are determined by market supply and demand conditions. Inflation expectations are the dominant factor behind Gilt yields. Gilts are essentially free of default risk and have active secondary and futures markets. Budget surpluses in the late 1980s led to a period of no Gilt issuance. Issuance was resumed in 1991.

United Kingdom: Long Bond Rate - 3 Month LIBOR

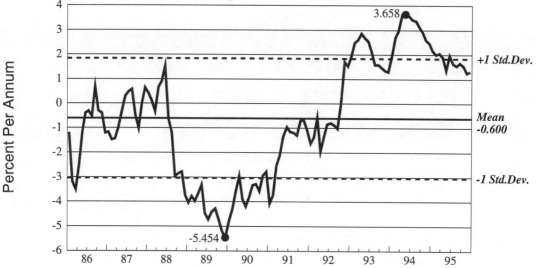

Source: Datastream

Date Range	Mean	Min.	Max.	Std.Dev.
1986-1995	-0.600	-5.454	3.658	2.440
1986	-1.164	-3.500	0.684	1.276
1987	-0.408	-1.481	0.644	0.801
1988	-0.902	-3.735	1.529	1.772
1989	-4.336	-5.454	-3.309	0.626
1990	-3.619	-4.776	-2.778	0.611
1991	-1.740	-4.071	-0.688	1.146
1992	-0.602	-1.945	1.698	1.151
1993	2.046	1.298	2.863	0.579
1994	3.034	1.962	3.658	0.535
1995	1.694	1.249	2.155	0.310

Financial assets are available in a range of maturities, from overnight to over 10 years. A yield curve compares yields at a given point in time across this maturity spectrum. Yields out the curve are essentially an average of what shorter-term rates are expected to be over the intervening period, say, the next 2 years, 5 years, or 10 years. So, the yield curve, whatever its shape may be at any given moment, indicates how the markets expect rates to move. And that, in turn, reveals a great deal about where the economy is headed, because expectations of what will happen to interest rates have a tremendous effect on the economy. A shorthand way to view the yield curve is by observing the behavior of the difference between the yield on a long-term security (usually a 10-year bond) and the yield on a short-term security (usually a 3-month deposit).

During an economic expansion (generally normal times), the market looks ahead and sees that continued economic growth is likely to push short rates higher than their current levels. Thus, the average of expected short rates will rise as we move further from the present. The result: long rates are higher than short rates--the yield curve is upward sloping. The opposite, a downward sloping yield curve, represents expectations that in the future short rates will be lower than they currently are. The yield curve's shape will also reflect supply/demand factors at different maturities.

The shift in Britain's yield curve from inverted to upward-sloping after the pound was withdrawn from the ERM in 1992 helped the U.K. move into an expansionary mode after a long recession. More recently, the curve has flattened as the Bank of England has been raising short term rates to fend off long term inflation.

PART 2
Foreign Interest Rates

SECTION III
Japan

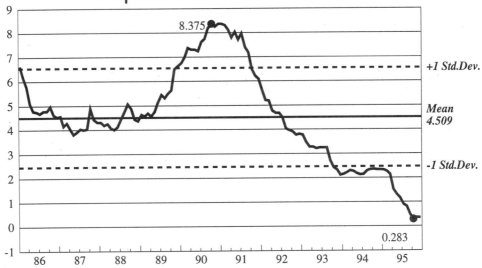

Date Range	Mean	Min.	Max.	Std.Dev.
1986-1995	4.509	0.283	8.375	2.038
1986	5.130	4.531	6.625	0.678
1987	4.203	3.813	4.875	0.305
1988	4.407	4.000	5.063	0.332
1989	5.276	4.563	6.625	0.714
1990	7.630	6.750	8.375	0.556
1991	7.479	6.094	8.375	0.808
1992	4.516	3.781	5.625	0.621
1993	3.034	2.125	3.781	0.505
1994	2.258	2.131	2.363	0.087
1995	1.161	0.283	2.328	0.765

Eurocurrency deposits/loans are bank liabilities/assets denominated in a foreign currency. The location of the bank accepting the deposit or making the loan is the determining factor. Japanese yen-denominated deposits in London, for example, are Euro-yen even if the depositor is a Japanese citizen and the bank is a London branch of a Japanese bank. These deposits have the same terms as those available for deposits denominated in the domestic currency; that is, funds may be placed for as short as overnight or as long as for 12 months. The interest rate obtained depends on market demand and supply and fluctuates daily. Rates are influenced primarily by the conditions prevailing in the respective domestic markets, the most important of which is the current stance of domestic monetary policy, and, to a lesser extent, by conditions in the foreign exchange markets. London is by far the largest market for Eurocurrency-denominated deposits and loans. The interest rate quoted for deposits, the London interbank offered rate (LIBOR), is frequently used as the benchmark short-term interest rate.

The Euro-yen market has grown rapidly due largely to the myriad of restrictions that the Japanese government continues to place on deposits held in domestic banks and the growing importance of the yen as a reserve currency, especially for newly industrialized Asian countries.

Date Range	Mean	Min.	Max.	Std.Dev.
1986-1995	4.492	0.266	8.563	2.014
1986	5.063	4.469	6.563	0.656
1987	4.208	3.781	5.000	0.315
1988	4.474	4.188	5.125	0.316
1989	5.328	4.563	6.625	0.678
1990	7.745	6.875	8.563	0.545
1991	7.227	5.844	7.938	0.800
1992	4.395	3.719	5.438	0.580
1993	3.005	1.969	3.719	0.527
1994	2.309	2.016	2.475	0.142
1995	1.162	0.266	2.377	0.764

Eurocurrency deposits/loans are bank liabilities/assets denominated in a foreign currency. The location of the bank accepting the deposit or making the loan is the determining factor. Japanese yen-denominated deposits in London, for example, are Euro-yen even if the depositor is a Japanese citizen and the bank is a London branch of a Japanese bank. These deposits have the same terms as those available for deposits denominated in the domestic currency; that is, funds may be placed for as short as overnight or as long as for 12 months. The interest rate obtained depends on market demand and supply and fluctuates daily. Rates are influenced primarily by the conditions prevailing in the respective domestic markets, the most important of which is the current stance of domestic monetary policy, and, to a lesser extent, by conditions in the foreign exchange markets. London is by far the largest market for Eurocurrency-denominated deposits and loans. The interest rate quoted for deposits, the London interbank offered rate (LIBOR), is frequently used as the benchmark short-term interest rate.

The Euro-yen market has grown rapidly due largely to the myriad of restrictions that the Japanese government continues to place on deposits held in domestic banks and the growing importance of the yen as a reserve currency, especially for newly industrialized Asian countries.

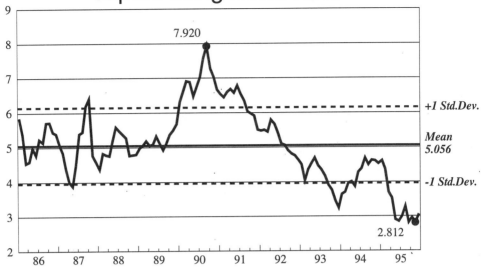

Date Range	Mean	Min.	Max.	Std.Dev.
1986-1995	5.056	2.812	7.920	1.097
1986	5.232	4.550	5.860	0.436
1987	4.952	3.880	6.401	0.790
1988	5.001	4.373	5.588	0.368
1989	5.198	4.924	5.680	0.224
1990	6.954	6.320	7.920	0.456
1991	6.332	5.510	6.780	0.383
1992	5.217	4.640	5.800	0.386
1993	4.123	3.237	4.690	0.455
1994	4.232	3.643	4.682	0.377
1995	3.321	2.812	4.613	0.616

Japanese Government Bonds (JGBs) are usually issued in denominations of 100,000 yen and traded on a simple yield basis. JGBs pay interest semi-annually on a 365-day year basis. Yields are determined by market supply and demand conditions with inflation expectations playing a dominant role. JGBs are essentially free of default risk and have active secondary and futures markets. The JGB market is the second largest bond market in the world.

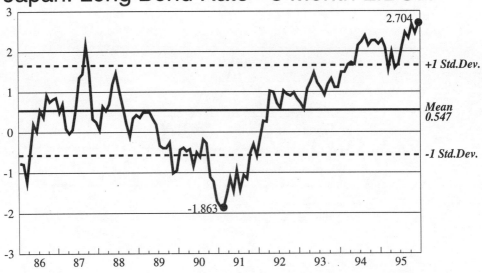

Date Range	Mean	Min.	Max.	Std.Dev.
1986-1995	0.547	-1.863	2.704	1.111
1986	0.102	-1.231	0.930	0.748
1987	0.748	-0.031	2.157	0.704
1988	0.595	-0.103	1.463	0.461
1989	-0.078	-1.010	0.493	0.550
1990	-0.676	-1.705	-0.180	0.454
1991	-1.148	-1.863	-0.299	0.502
1992	0.701	-0.145	1.029	0.379
1993	1.089	0.571	1.471	0.250
1994	1.974	1.486	2.387	0.335
1995	2.160	1.560	2.704	0.397

Source: Datastream

Financial assets are available in a range of maturities, from overnight to over 10 years. A yield curve compares yields at a given point in time across this maturity spectrum. Yields out the curve are essentially an average of what shorter-term rates are expected to be over the intervening period, say, the next 2 years, 5 years, or 10 years. So, the yield curve, whatever its shape may be at any given moment, indicates how the markets expect rates to move. And that, in turn, reveals a great deal about where the economy is headed, because expectations of what will happen to interest rates have a tremendous effect on the economy. A shorthand way to view the yield curve is by observing the behavior of the difference between the yield on a long-term security (usually a 10-year bond) and the yield on a short-term security (usually a 3-month deposit).

During an economic expansion (generally normal times), the market looks ahead and sees that continued economic growth is likely to push short rates higher than their current levels. Thus, the average of expected short rates will rise as we move further from the present. The result: long rates are higher than short rates--the yield curve is upward sloping. The opposite, a downward sloping yield curve, represents expectations that in the future short rates will be lower than they currently are. The yield curve's shape will also reflect supply/demand factors at different maturities.

Japan's yield curve is currently upward sloping, reflecting the Bank of Japan's attempts to boost the Japanese economy, which has been in recession since 1992. Recent steepening of the Japanese yield curve reflects long term rates moving along with other international government bond markets.

PART 2
Foreign Interest Rates

SECTION IV
Switzerland

Switzerland: 3 Month LIBOR

Source: Datastream

Date Range	Mean	Min.	Max.	Std.Dev.
1986-1995	5.519	1.750	9.625	2.228
1986	4.224	3.813	5.063	0.395
1987	3.849	3.500	4.313	0.216
1988	3.120	1.750	4.688	0.975
1989	6.880	4.750	8.000	1.063
1990	8.901	7.938	9.625	0.473
1991	8.221	7.875	8.688	0.261
1992	7.932	6.375	9.375	1.032
1993	4.958	4.438	5.938	0.439
1994	4.098	3.918	4.277	0.113
1995	3.007	1.988	4.043	0.688

Eurocurrency deposits/loans are bank liabilities/assets denominated in a foreign currency. The location of the bank accepting the deposit or making the loan is the determining factor. Swiss franc-denominated deposits in London, for example, are Euro-Swiss francs even if the depositor is a Swiss citizen and the bank is a London branch of a Swiss bank. These deposits have the same terms as those available for deposits denominated in the domestic currency; that is, funds may be placed for as short as overnight or for as long as 12 months. The interest rate obtained depends on market demand and supply and fluctuates daily. Rates are influenced primarily by the conditions prevailing in the respective domestic markets, the most important of which is the current stance of domestic monetary policy, and, to a lesser extent, by conditions in the foreign exchange markets. London is by far the largest market for Eurocurrency-denominated deposits and loans. The interest rate quoted for deposits, the London interbank offered rate (LIBOR), is frequently used as the benchmark short-term interest rate.

The size of the Euro-Swiss franc market is much larger than the relative importance of the Swiss economy, owing to its "safe-haven status" and the political stability often associated with the Swiss franc.

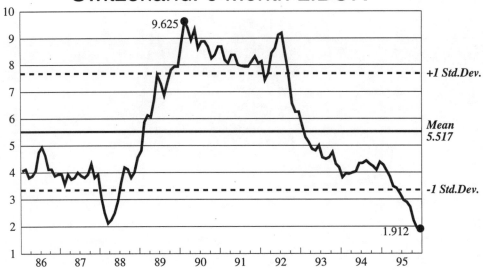

Switzerland: 6 Month LIBOR

Source: Datastream

Date Range	Mean	Min.	Max.	Std.Dev.
1986-1995	5.517	1.912	9.625	2.168
1986	4.193	3.813	4.938	0.371
1987	3.891	3.563	4.313	0.177
1988	3.308	2.125	4.563	0.846
1989	6.870	4.813	7.938	0.984
1990	8.870	8.250	9.625	0.403
1991	8.169	7.938	8.688	0.229
1992	7.818	6.250	9.188	1.034
1993	4.813	4.188	5.750	0.440
1994	4.159	3.816	4.435	0.207
1995	3.083	1.912	4.281	0.790

Eurocurrency deposits/loans are bank liabilities/assets denominated in a foreign currency. The location of the bank accepting the deposit or making the loan is the determining factor. Swiss franc-denominated deposits in London, for example, are Euro-Swiss francs even if the depositor is a Swiss citizen and the bank is a London branch of a Swiss bank. These deposits have the same terms as those available for deposits denominated in the domestic currency; that is, funds may be placed for as short as overnight or for as long as 12 months. The interest rate obtained depends on market demand and supply and fluctuates daily. Rates are influenced primarily by the conditions prevailing in the respective domestic markets, the most important of which is the current stance of domestic monetary policy, and, to a lesser extent, by conditions in the foreign exchange markets. London is by far the largest market for Eurocurrency-denominated deposits and loans. The interest rate quoted for deposits, the London interbank offered rate (LIBOR), is frequently used as the benchmark short-term interest rate.

The size of the Euro-Swiss franc market is much larger than the relative importance of the Swiss economy, owing to its "safe-haven status" and the political stability often associated with the Swiss franc.

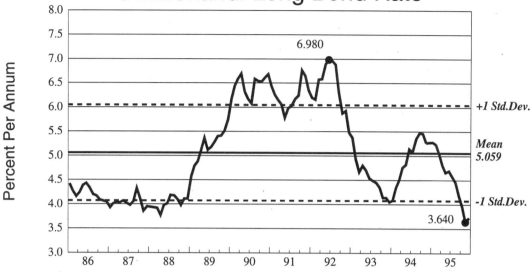

Source: Datastream

Date Range	Mean	Min.	Max.	Std.Dev.
1986-1995	5.059	3.640	6.980	0.987
1986	4.236	4.050	4.430	0.136
1987	4.033	3.860	4.330	0.116
1988	4.018	3.770	4.190	0.123
1989	5.198	4.580	5.750	0.328
1990	6.450	6.080	6.690	0.212
1991	6.239	5.790	6.760	0.277
1992	6.401	5.480	6.980	0.489
1993	4.553	4.050	5.370	0.376
1994	4.934	4.080	5.470	0.472
1995	4.522	3.640	5.280	0.549

Swiss federal government bonds can vary in maturity from one to twenty-one years and are issued in denominations of Sfr 5,000 and Sfr 100,000. All currently outstanding bonds are fixed-coupons; about 80% are callable, while the remainder are in bullet form. They are issued by tender through a Swiss bank. Interest is paid semi-annually on a 30/360 day year basis and is subject to a 35% withholding tax. Yields are generally determined by market demand and supply conditions with inflation expectations playing the dominant role. Swiss government bonds are essentially free of default risk and have active secondary and futures markets.

FOREIGN INTEREST RATES

Switzerland: Long Bond Rate - 3 Month LIBOR

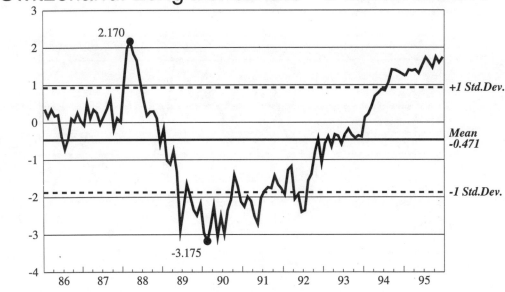

Date Range	Mean	Min.	Max.	Std.Dev.
1986-1995	-0.471	-3.175	2.170	1.401
1986	0.012	-0.723	0.358	0.340
1987	0.184	-0.193	0.642	0.249
1988	0.898	-0.578	2.170	0.879
1989	-1.683	-2.880	-0.170	0.809
1990	-2.451	-3.175	-1.408	0.563
1991	-1.982	-2.710	-1.428	0.366
1992	-1.531	-2.395	-0.445	0.611
1993	-0.406	-0.642	-0.175	0.132
1994	0.839	0.136	1.408	0.450
1995	1.514	1.237	1.750	0.175

Financial assets are available in a range of maturities, from overnight to over 10 years. A yield curve compares yields at a given point in time across this maturity spectrum. Yields out the curve are essentially an average of what shorter-term rates are expected to be over the intervening period, say, the next 2 years, 5 years, or 10 years. So, the yield curve, whatever its shape may be at any given moment, indicates how the markets expect rates to move. And that, in turn, reveals a great deal about where the economy is headed, because expectations of what will happen to interest rates have a tremendous effect on the economy. A shorthand way to view the yield curve is by observing the behavior of the difference between the yield on a long-term security (usually a 10-year bond) and the yield on a short-term security (usually a 3-month deposit).

During an economic expansion (generally normal times), the market looks ahead and sees that continued economic growth is likely to push short rates higher than their current levels. Thus, the average of expected short rates will rise as we move further from the present. The result: long rates are higher than short rates--the yield curve is upward sloping. The opposite, a downward sloping yield curve, represents expectations that in the future short rates will be lower than they currently are. The yield curve's shape will also reflect supply/demand factors at different maturities.

Reflecting the low inflation environment that has characterized the Swiss economy, the Swiss yield curve has normally been flat. Recent steepening of the yield curve reflects Swiss long term rates moving up along with those of other international government bonds.

PART 2
Foreign Interest Rates

SECTION V
France

France: 3 Month LIBOR

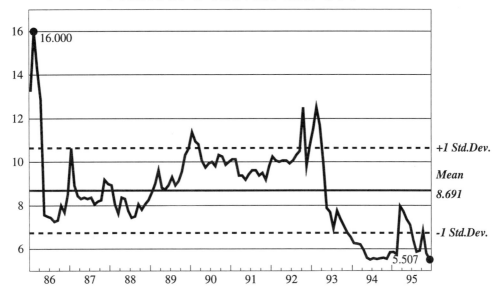

Date Range	Mean	Min.	Max.	Std.Dev.
1986-1995	8.691	5.507	16.000	1.955
1986	9.802	7.250	16.000	3.269
1987	8.672	8.063	10.625	0.709
1988	8.016	7.438	8.938	0.426
1989	9.302	8.625	10.625	0.628
1990	10.260	9.750	11.375	0.513
1991	9.563	9.188	10.125	0.318
1992	10.359	9.813	12.500	0.722
1993	8.641	6.563	12.500	2.161
1994	5.789	5.517	6.265	0.302
1995	6.510	5.507	7.965	0.854

Eurocurrency deposits/loans are bank liabilities/assets denominated in a foreign currency. The location of the bank accepting the deposit or making the loan is the determining factor. French franc-denominated deposits in London, for example, are Euro-French francs even if the depositor is a French citizen and the bank is a London branch of a French bank. These deposits have the same terms as those available for deposits denominated in the domestic currency; that is, funds may be placed for as short as overnight or for as long as 12 months. The interest rate obtained depends on market demand and supply and fluctuates daily. Rates are influenced primarily by the conditions prevailing in the respective domestic markets, the most important of which is the current stance of domestic monetary policy, and, to a lesser extent, by conditions in the foreign exchange markets. London is by far the largest market for Eurocurrency-denominated deposits and loans. The interest rate quoted for deposits, the London interbank offered rate (LIBOR), is frequently used as the benchmark short-term interest rate.

Until about five years ago, Euro-French franc rates were above comparable domestic rates. This difference generally reflected controls on capital flows into and out of France that have now been eliminated. Spikes in French rates during 1992 and 1993 were associated with attempts to ward off speculative attacks against the French franc. However, since mid-1993, Euro-French franc rates have been low and stable, reflecting low inflation and relative calm in the European currency markets.

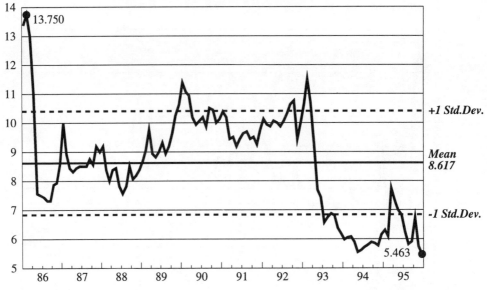

France: 6 Month LIBOR

Date Range	Mean	Min.	Max.	Std.Dev.
1986-1995	8.617	5.463	13.750	1.783
1986	9.385	7.313	13.750	2.610
1987	8.761	8.313	10.000	0.473
1988	8.224	7.563	9.188	0.423
1989	9.349	8.688	10.625	0.601
1990	10.391	9.875	11.375	0.488
1991	9.615	9.188	10.375	0.352
1992	10.089	9.438	10.750	0.348
1993	8.063	6.188	11.500	1.919
1994	5.862	5.543	6.151	0.187
1995	6.431	5.463	7.745	0.696

Eurocurrency deposits/loans are bank liabilities/assets denominated in a foreign currency. The location of the bank accepting the deposit or making the loan is the determining factor. French franc-denominated deposits in London, for example, are Euro-French francs even if the depositor is a French citizen and the bank is a London branch of a French bank. These deposits have the same terms as those available for deposits denominated in the domestic currency; that is, funds may be placed for as short as overnight or for as long as 12 months. The interest rate obtained depends on market demand and supply and fluctuates daily. Rates are influenced primarily by the conditions prevailing in the respective domestic markets, the most important of which is the current stance of domestic monetary policy, and, to a lesser extent, by conditions in the foreign exchange markets. London is by far the largest market for Eurocurrency-denominated deposits and loans. The interest rate quoted for deposits, the London interbank offered rate (LIBOR), is frequently used as the benchmark short-term interest rate.

Until about five years ago, Euro-French franc rates were above comparable domestic rates. This difference generally reflected controls on capital flows into and out of France that have now been eliminated. Spikes in French rates during 1992 and 1993 were associated with attempts to ward off speculative attacks against the French franc. However, since mid-1993, Euro-French franc rates have been low and stable, reflecting low inflation and relative calm in the European currency markets.

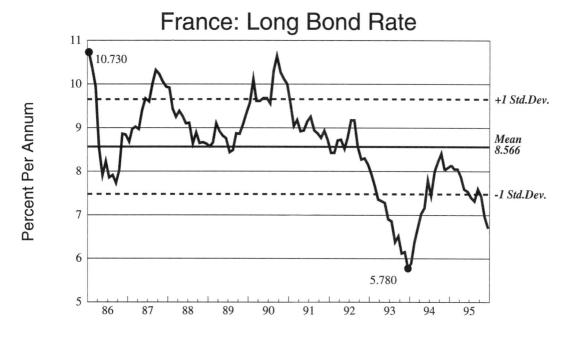

Date Range	Mean	Min.	Max.	Std.Dev.
1986-1995	8.566	5.780	10.730	1.087
1986	8.744	7.730	10.730	1.048
1987	9.573	8.680	10.320	0.559
1988	9.079	8.640	9.920	0.400
1989	8.825	8.440	9.340	0.265
1990	9.929	9.560	10.640	0.360
1991	9.021	8.720	9.550	0.230
1992	8.605	8.160	9.170	0.326
1993	6.857	5.780	7.940	0.676
1994	7.367	5.890	8.410	0.813
1995	7.555	6.700	8.140	0.438

The most popular French long-term bond is the OAT (obligation assimilable du Tresor), representing most of the French government's long-term debt. Their maturities range from seven to 30 years, but the most popular maturity is the 10 year. They are denominated in units of Ffr 2,000. Interest on fixed-rate OATs is paid annually based on an Actual/Actual day year. Yields are determined based on market demand and supply conditions with inflation expectations playing a dominant role in determining OAT yields. OATs are essentially free of default risk and have active secondary and futures markets.

Date Range	Mean	Min.	Max.	Std.Dev.
1986-1995	-0.150	-5.630	2.818	1.601
1986	-1.058	-5.630	1.173	2.431
1987	0.901	-1.945	2.132	1.092
1988	1.063	0.390	1.672	0.388
1989	-0.477	-1.285	0.107	0.470
1990	-0.331	-1.805	0.488	0.671
1991	-0.542	-1.093	-0.195	0.307
1992	-1.754	-4.220	-0.892	0.895
1993	-1.784	-4.830	-0.077	1.629
1994	1.584	-0.375	2.818	1.104
1995	1.045	0.085	2.303	0.776

Financial assets are available in a range of maturities, from overnight to 10 years or more. A yield curve compares yields at a given point in time across this maturity spectrum. Yields out the curve are essentially an average of what shorter-term rates are expected to be over the intervening period, say, the next 2 years, 5 years, or 10 years. So, the yield curve, whatever its shape may be at any given moment, indicates how the markets expect rates to move. And that, in turn, reveals a great deal about where the economy is headed, because expectations of what will happen to interest rates have a tremendous effect on the economy. A shorthand way to view the yield curve is by observing the behavior of the difference between the yield on a long-term security (usually a 10-year bond) and the yield on a short-term security (usually a 3-month deposit).

During an economic expansion (generally normal times), the market looks ahead and sees that continued economic growth is likely to push short rates higher than their current levels. Thus, the average of expected short rates will rise as we move further from the present. The result: long rates are higher than short rates--the yield curve is upward sloping. The opposite, a downward sloping yield curve, represents expectations that in the future short rates will be lower than they currently are. The yield curve's shape will also reflect supply/demand factors at different maturities.

The French yield curve changed from inverted to normal during the course of 1994 as short term rates fell, reflecting a more accommodative monetary policy and long term rates rose along with other international markets and due to an increasing French budget deficit.

PART 2
Foreign Interest Rates

SECTION VI
Italy

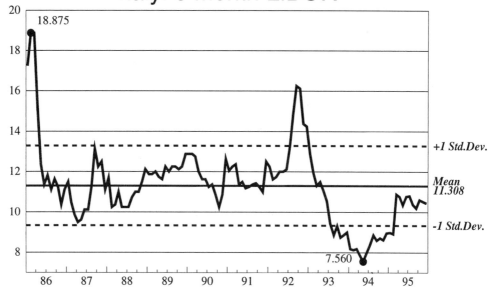

Italy: 3 Month LIBOR

Date Range	Mean	Min.	Max.	Std.Dev.
1986-1995	11.308	7.560	18.875	1.967
1986	13.443	10.375	18.875	3.207
1987	10.958	9.500	13.125	1.199
1988	10.870	10.250	12.125	0.639
1989	12.094	11.625	12.875	0.325
1990	11.750	10.250	12.875	0.882
1991	11.630	11.000	12.500	0.518
1992	13.406	11.625	16.250	1.710
1993	10.292	8.750	12.875	1.424
1994	8.333	7.560	8.966	0.430
1995	10.306	8.919	10.886	0.666

Eurocurrency deposits/loans are bank liabilities/assets denominated in a foreign currency. The location of the bank accepting the deposit or making the loan is the determining factor. Italian lira-denominated deposits in London, for example, are Euro-lira even if the depositor is an Italian citizen and the bank is a London branch of an Italian bank. These deposits have the same terms as those available for deposits denominated in the domestic currency; that is, funds may be placed for as short as overnight or for as long as 12 months. The interest rate obtained depends on market demand and supply and fluctuates daily. Rates are influenced primarily by the conditions prevailing in the respective domestic markets, the most important of which is the current stance of domestic monetary policy, and, to a lesser extent, by conditions in the foreign exchange markets. London is by far the largest market for Eurocurrency-denominated deposits and loans. The interest rate quoted for deposits, the London interbank offered rate (LIBOR), is frequently used as the benchmark short-term interest rate.

The Euro-lira market is relatively small, reflecting the minor role that the lira plays outside of the Italian economy and the general political uncertainty associated with investing in lira-denominated assets.

FOREIGN INTEREST RATES

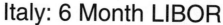
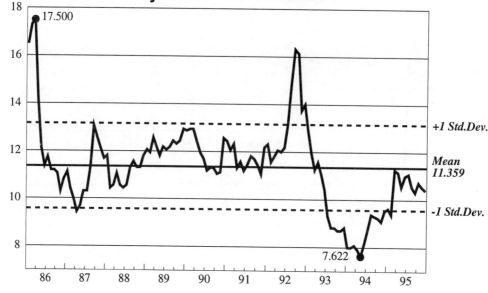

Date Range	Mean	Min.	Max.	Std.Dev.
1986-1995	11.359	7.622	17.500	1.801
1986	12.948	10.313	17.500	2.696
1987	11.005	9.438	13.063	1.167
1988	11.063	10.438	11.813	0.530
1989	12.261	11.813	12.938	0.304
1990	11.948	11.063	12.938	0.760
1991	11.708	11.063	12.438	0.455
1992	13.349	11.563	16.313	1.675
1993	10.188	8.688	12.875	1.510
1994	8.572	7.622	9.514	0.686
1995	10.546	9.378	11.261	0.578

Eurocurrency deposits/loans are bank liabilities/assets denominated in a foreign currency. The location of the bank accepting the deposit or making the loan is the determining factor. Italian lira-denominated deposits in London, for example, are Euro-lira even if the depositor is an Italian citizen and the bank is a London branch of an Italian bank. These deposits have the same terms as those available for deposits denominated in the domestic currency; that is, funds may be placed for as short as overnight or for as long as 12 months. The interest rate obtained depends on market demand and supply and fluctuates daily. Rates are influenced primarily by the conditions prevailing in the respective domestic markets, the most important of which is the current stance of domestic monetary policy, and, to a lesser extent, by conditions in the foreign exchange markets. London is by far the largest market for Eurocurrency-denominated deposits and loans. The interest rate quoted for deposits, the London interbank offered rate (LIBOR), is frequently used as the benchmark short-term interest rate.

The Euro-lira market is relatively small, reflecting the minor role that the lira plays outside of the Italian economy and the general political uncertainty associated with investing in lira-denominated assets.

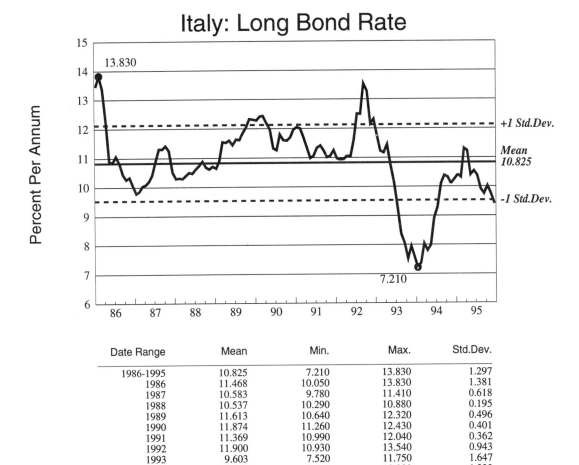

Date Range	Mean	Min.	Max.	Std.Dev.
1986-1995	10.825	7.210	13.830	1.297
1986	11.468	10.050	13.830	1.381
1987	10.583	9.780	11.410	0.618
1988	10.537	10.290	10.880	0.195
1989	11.613	10.640	12.320	0.496
1990	11.874	11.260	12.430	0.401
1991	11.369	10.990	12.040	0.362
1992	11.900	10.930	13.540	0.943
1993	9.603	7.520	11.750	1.647
1994	8.865	7.210	10.380	1.233
1995	10.281	9.400	11.300	0.569

The fixed-rate Italian government bond is the BTP (Buoni del Tresoro Poliennali). It is usually issued with 5-, 8-, or 10-year maturities. Interest is paid semi-annually on a 30/360 basis (and is subject to a 12.5% withholding tax) with bullet repayments of principal at maturity. BTPs are issued by Dutch auction. Yields are generally determined by market supply and demand conditions; inflation expectations are one of the most important factors behind BTP yields. BTPs have active secondary and futures markets.

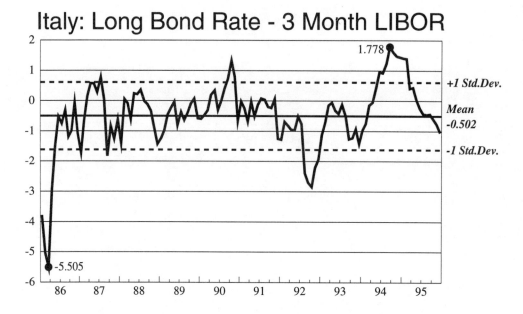

Date Range	Mean	Min.	Max.	Std.Dev.
1986-1995	-0.502	-5.505	1.778	1.116
1986	-1.975	-5.505	-0.045	1.880
1987	-0.375	-1.825	0.775	0.908
1988	-0.333	-1.425	0.360	0.617
1989	-0.481	-1.235	0.070	0.393
1990	0.124	-0.665	1.330	0.626
1991	-0.261	-1.250	0.080	0.388
1992	-1.506	-2.845	-0.515	0.856
1993	-0.689	-1.420	-0.060	0.491
1994	0.589	-0.974	1.778	0.956
1995	-0.025	-1.044	1.409	0.797

Financial assets are available in a range of maturities, from overnight to 10 years or more. A yield curve compares yields at a given point in time across this maturity spectrum. Yields out the curve are essentially an average of what shorter-term rates are expected to be over the intervening period, say, the next 2 years, 5 years, or 10 years. So, the yield curve, whatever its shape may be at any given moment, indicates how the markets expect rates to move. And that, in turn, reveals a great deal about where the economy is headed, because expectations of what will happen to interest rates have a tremendous effect on the economy. A shorthand way to view the yield curve is by observing the behavior of the difference between the yield on a long-term security (usually a 10-year bond) and the yield on a short-term security (usually a 3-month deposit).

During an economic expansion (generally normal times), the market looks ahead and sees that continued economic growth is likely to push short rates higher than their current levels. Thus, the average of expected short rates will rise as we move further from the present. The result: long rates are higher than short rates--the yield curve is upward sloping. The opposite, a downward sloping yield curve, represents expectations that in the future short rates will be lower than they currently are. The yield curve's shape will also reflect supply/demand factors at different maturities.

The Italian yield curve has normally been inverted, reflecting the market's skepticism that short-term interest rates can remain at current levels. However, the curve is positively sloped at present, reflecting lower short term rates due to improvements in inflation and higher long term rates, which have risen with other international markets and with increased political uncertainty.

PART 2
Foreign Interest Rates

SECTION VII
Canada

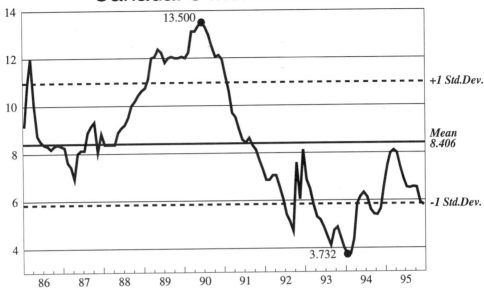

Canada: 3 Month LIBOR

Date Range	Mean	Min.	Max.	Std.Dev.
1986-1995	8.406	3.732	13.500	2.561
1986	9.099	8.188	12.000	1.233
1987	8.224	6.938	9.313	0.707
1988	9.281	8.375	10.625	0.855
1989	11.875	10.750	12.375	0.466
1990	12.693	11.938	13.500	0.601
1991	8.927	7.313	11.250	1.161
1992	6.461	4.719	8.125	1.017
1993	5.104	4.000	6.875	0.897
1994	5.416	3.732	6.591	0.968
1995	6.975	5.792	8.095	0.798

Eurocurrency deposits/loans are bank liabilities/assets denominated in a foreign currency. The location of the bank accepting the deposit or making the loan is the determining factor. Canadian dollar-denominated deposits in London, for example, are Euro-Canadian dollars even if the depositor is a Canadian citizen and the bank is a London branch of a Canadian bank. These deposits have the same terms as those available for deposits denominated in the domestic currency; that is, funds may be placed for as short as overnight or for as long as 12 months. The interest rate obtained depends on market demand and supply and fluctuates daily. Rates are influenced primarily by the conditions prevailing in the respective domestic markets, the most important of which is the current stance of domestic monetary policy, and, to a lesser extent, by conditions in the foreign exchange markets. London is by far the largest market for Eurocurrency-denominated deposits and loans. The interest rate quoted for deposits, the London interbank offered rate (LIBOR), is frequently used as the benchmark short-term interest rate.

The rather limited role of the Canadian dollar in the world's currency markets keeps the Euro-Canadian dollar market relatively small.

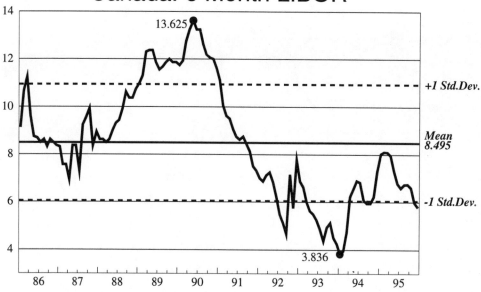

Date Range	Mean	Min.	Max.	Std.Dev.
1986-1995	8.495	3.836	13.625	2.449
1986	9.089	8.313	11.250	0.955
1987	8.375	6.938	9.938	0.927
1988	9.516	8.500	10.750	0.860
1989	11.844	11.000	12.375	0.417
1990	12.526	11.625	13.625	0.688
1991	8.906	7.313	11.125	1.071
1992	6.430	4.656	7.750	0.972
1993	5.328	4.250	6.875	0.842
1994	5.875	3.836	7.290	1.124
1995	7.063	5.783	8.106	0.822

Eurocurrency deposits/loans are bank liabilities/assets denominated in a foreign currency. The location of the bank accepting the deposit or making the loan is the determining factor. Canadian dollar-denominated deposits in London, for example, are Euro-Canadian dollars even if the depositor is a Canadian citizen and the bank is a London branch of a Canadian bank. These deposits have the same terms as those available for deposits denominated in the domestic currency, that is, funds may be placed for as short as overnight or as long as for 12 months. The interest rate obtained depends on market demand and supply and fluctuates daily. Rates are influenced primarily by the conditions prevailing in the respective domestic markets, the most important of which is the current stance of domestic monetary policy, and to a lesser extent by conditions in the foreign exchange markets. London is by far the largest market for Eurocurrency-denominated deposits and loans. The interest rate quoted for deposits, the London interbank offered rate (LIBOR), is frequently used as the benchmark short-term interest rate.

The rather limited role of the Canadian dollar in the world's currency markets keeps the Euro-Canadian dollar market relatively small.

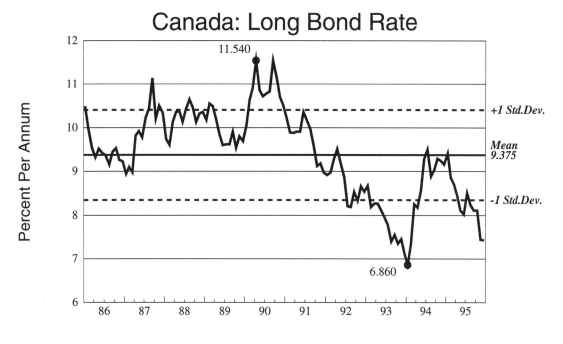

Date Range	Mean	Min.	Max.	Std.Dev.
1986-1995	9.375	6.860	11.540	1.031
1986	9.520	9.160	10.490	0.369
1987	9.950	8.940	11.140	0.673
1988	10.224	9.610	10.650	0.299
1989	9.920	9.540	10.550	0.352
1990	10.852	10.040	11.540	0.416
1991	9.764	8.970	10.360	0.453
1992	8.765	8.190	9.510	0.427
1993	7.845	7.120	8.670	0.473
1994	8.632	6.860	9.500	0.836
1995	8.281	7.430	9.410	0.560

Canadian government bonds can vary in maturity from one to 30 years and are issued in denominations of C$1,000. Trading lots are normally C$10 million. Interest is paid semi-annually based on an Actual/Actual day year. Canadian government bonds are issued by auction. Yields are generally determined by market demand and supply conditions, with inflation expectations playing the dominant role. Canadian government bonds are essentially free of default risk and have active secondary and futures markets.

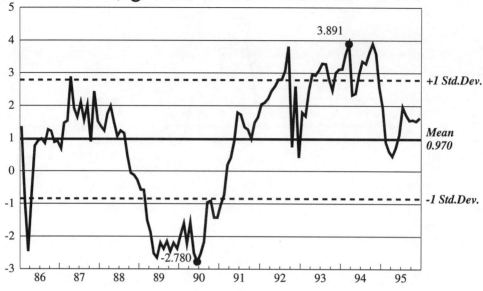

Date Range	Mean	Min.	Max.	Std.Dev.
1986-1995	0.970	-2.780	3.891	1.818
1986	0.421	-2.460	1.365	1.168
1987	1.726	0.690	2.883	0.606
1988	0.943	-0.265	1.985	0.756
1989	-1.955	-2.650	-0.570	0.714
1990	-1.841	-2.780	-0.913	0.616
1991	0.837	-1.030	1.798	0.947
1992	2.304	0.415	3.811	0.939
1993	2.741	1.690	3.290	0.536
1994	3.215	2.335	3.891	0.551
1995	1.306	0.456	1.961	0.530

Financial assets are available in a range of maturities, from overnight to 10 years or more. A yield curve compares yields at a given point in time across this maturity spectrum. Yields out the curve are essentially an average of what shorter-term rates are expected to be over the intervening period, say, the next 2 years, 5 years, or 10 years. So, the yield curve, whatever its shape may be at any given moment, indicates how the markets expect rates to move. And that, in turn, reveals a great deal about where the economy is headed, because expectations of what will happen to interest rates have a tremendous effect on the economy. A shorthand way to view the yield curve is by observing the behavior of the difference between the yield on a long-term security (usually a 10-year bond) and the yield on a short-term security (usually a 3-month deposit).

During an economic expansion (generally normal times), the market looks ahead and sees that continued economic growth is likely to push short rates higher than their current levels. Thus, the average of expected short rates will rise as we move further from the present. The result: long rates are higher than short rates--the yield curve is upward sloping. The opposite, a downward sloping yield curve, represents expectations that in the future short rates will be lower than they currently are. The yield curve's shape will also reflect supply/demand factors at different maturities.

The current upward sloping yield curve clearly reveals a monetary policy supportive of economic recovery.

PART 3
Foreign Exchange Rates

SECTION I
Spot Rates versus Purchasing Power Parity

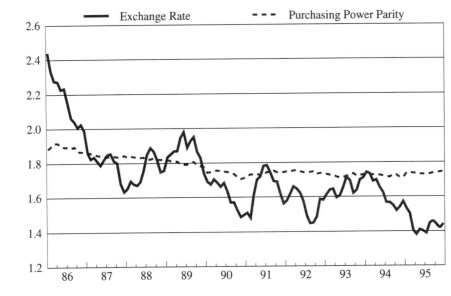

Deutsche Mark Exchange Rate

Date Range	Mean	Min.	Max.	Std.Dev.
1986-1995	1.717	1.381	2.438	0.209
1986	2.171	1.988	2.438	0.147
1987	1.798	1.634	1.860	0.070
1988	1.756	1.654	1.888	0.081
1989	1.879	1.738	1.979	0.066
1990	1.616	1.486	1.705	0.081
1991	1.659	1.481	1.785	0.101
1992	1.562	1.448	1.662	0.075
1993	1.654	1.596	1.716	0.042
1994	1.622	1.520	1.743	0.080
1995	1.435	1.381	1.530	0.047

This foreign exchange rate is freely determined by demand and supply conditions in the FX markets, but the Federal Reserve and the Central Bank of Germany (Bundesbank) can intervene in these markets when necessary. Germany is a member of the exchange rate mechanism (ERM) of the European Monetary System; therefore, the Bundesbank has an obligation to sell or buy Deutsche Marks against the currencies of the other members of the ERM (Belgium, Denmark, France, Ireland, Luxembourg, the Netherlands, Portugal and Spain) in order to keep these exchange rates within a pre-established range.

The purchasing power parity (PPP) theory states that at the equilibrium level, the exchange rate between the Deutsche Mark and the U.S. Dollar should be equal to the ratio of Germany's and the United States' price levels. To calculate PPP, we begin with the base period of 1978-81, in which currencies were "correctly valued" (defined as a time when the current account balances of the three biggest industrial nations - the United States, Germany and Japan - were close to equilibrium). To calculate PPP for future periods, the base-PPP is simply adjusted for inflation differentials, using producer price inflation as a measure of inflation.

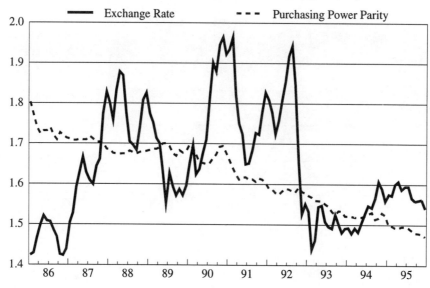

Date Range	Mean	Min.	Max.	Std.Dev.
1986-1995	1.646	1.424	1.964	0.142
1986	1.467	1.424	1.521	0.037
1987	1.639	1.505	1.829	0.091
1988	1.781	1.684	1.878	0.066
1989	1.640	1.553	1.774	0.076
1990	1.785	1.625	1.964	0.132
1991	1.770	1.650	1.964	0.102
1992	1.764	1.527	1.943	0.132
1993	1.502	1.440	1.548	0.033
1994	1.532	1.479	1.606	0.043
1995	1.578	1.541	1.607	0.020

This foreign exchange rate is freely determined by demand and supply conditions in the FX markets, but the Federal Reserve and the Bank of England can intervene in these markets when necessary, selling or buying the Pound Sterling against any convertible currency. Sterling participated in the exchange rate mechanism of the European Monetary System between October 1990 and September 1992.

The purchasing power parity (PPP) theory states that at the equilibrium level, the exchange rate between the Pound Sterling and the U.S. Dollar should be equal to the ratio of the United Kingdom's and the United States' price levels. To calculate PPP, we begin with the base period of 1978-81, in which currencies were "correctly valued" (defined as a time when the current account balances of the three biggest industrial nations - the United States, Germany and Japan - were close to equilibrium). To calculate PPP for future periods, the base-PPP is simply adjusted for inflation differentials, using producer price inflation as a measure of inflation.

Date Range	Mean	Min.	Max.	Std.Dev.
1986-1995	129.527	83.690	199.890	22.233
1986	168.498	154.180	199.890	13.862
1987	144.631	128.240	154.830	7.651
1988	128.144	123.200	134.320	3.854
1989	137.995	127.360	145.070	6.701
1990	144.818	129.220	158.460	9.923
1991	134.508	128.040	139.750	3.917
1992	126.748	121.170	133.540	3.898
1993	111.231	103.770	124.990	6.476
1994	102.194	98.040	111.440	4.066
1995	93.495	83.690	101.940	7.384

This foreign exchange rate is freely determined by demand and supply conditions in the FX markets, but the Federal Reserve and the Bank of Japan can intervene in these markets when necessary, selling or buying Japanese Yen against any convertible currency (usually U.S. Dollars).

The purchasing power parity (PPP) theory states that at the equilibrium level, the exchange rate between the Japanese Yen and the U.S. Dollar should be equal to the ratio of Japan's and the United States' price levels. To calculate PPP, we begin with the base period of 1978-81, in which currencies were "correctly valued" (defined as a time when the current account balances of the three biggest industrial nations - the United States, Germany and Japan - were close to equilibrium). To calculate PPP for future periods, the base-PPP is simply adjusted for inflation differentials, using export prices as a measure of inflation.

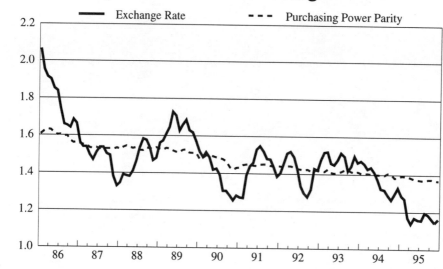

Date Range	Mean	Min.	Max.	Std.Dev.
1986-1995	1.467	1.138	2.066	0.173
1986	1.799	1.643	2.066	0.142
1987	1.492	1.330	1.562	0.069
1988	1.463	1.347	1.584	0.081
1989	1.635	1.562	1.729	0.054
1990	1.390	1.257	1.518	0.099
1991	1.434	1.269	1.548	0.092
1992	1.407	1.278	1.519	0.083
1993	1.478	1.418	1.521	0.032
1994	1.367	1.265	1.472	0.072
1995	1.185	1.138	1.286	0.049

This foreign exchange rate is freely determined by demand and supply conditions in the FX markets, but the Federal Reserve and the Swiss National Bank can intervene in these markets when necessary, selling or buying Swiss Francs against any convertible currency (usually U.S. Dollars).

The purchasing power parity (PPP) theory states that at the equilibrium level, the exchange rate between the Swiss Franc and the U.S. Dollar should be equal to the ratio of Switzerland's and the United States' price levels. To calculate PPP, we begin with the base period of 1978-81, in which currencies were "correctly valued" (defined as a time when the current account balances of the three biggest industrial nations - the United States, Germany and Japan - were close to equilibrium). To calculate PPP for future periods, the base-PPP is simply adjusted for inflation differentials, using producer price inflation as a measure of inflation.

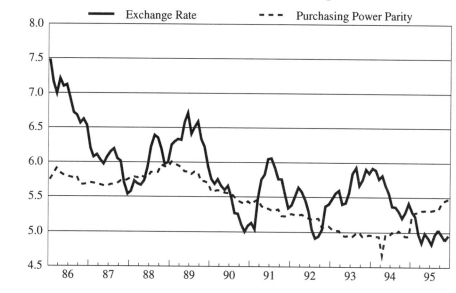

Date Range	Mean	Min.	Max.	Std.Dev.
1986-1995	5.792	4.831	7.482	0.582
1986	6.926	6.530	7.482	0.301
1987	6.011	5.538	6.201	0.197
1988	5.956	5.581	6.392	0.282
1989	6.375	5.939	6.714	0.205
1990	5.445	5.002	5.757	0.283
1991	5.639	5.040	6.060	0.337
1992	5.296	4.912	5.640	0.253
1993	5.664	5.398	5.930	0.190
1994	5.547	5.202	5.921	0.258
1995	4.994	4.831	5.291	0.145

This foreign exchange rate is freely determined by demand and supply conditions in the FX markets, but the Federal Reserve and Central Bank of France can intervene in these markets when necessary. France is a member of the exchange rate mechanism (ERM) of the European Monetary System; therefore, the Bank of France has an obligation to sell or buy Francs against the currencies of the other members of the ERM (Belgium, Denmark, Germany, Ireland, Luxembourg, the Netherlands, Portugal and Spain) in order to keep these exchange rates within a pre-established range.

The purchasing power parity (PPP) theory states that at the equilibrium level, the exchange rate between the French Franc and the U.S. Dollar should be equal to the ratio of France's and the United States' price levels. To calculate PPP, we begin with the base period of 1978-81, in which currencies were "correctly valued" (defined as a time when the current account balances of the three biggest industrial nations - the United States, Germany and Japan - were close to equilibrium). To calculate PPP for future periods, the base-PPP is simply adjusted for inflation differentials, using producer price inflation as a measure of inflation.

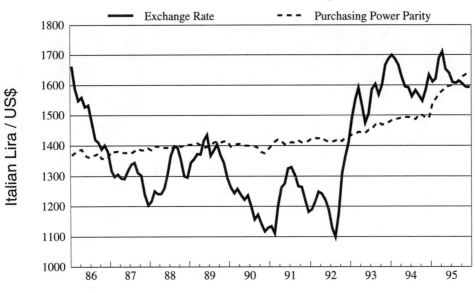

Italian Lira Exchange Rate

Date Range	Mean	Min.	Max.	Std.Dev.
1986-1995	1392.679	1100.000	1710.890	169.628
1986	1491.491	1379.440	1663.140	92.012
1987	1296.607	1203.740	1344.180	39.452
1988	1301.672	1216.880	1397.930	63.102
1989	1371.312	1291.930	1434.400	37.210
1990	1198.053	1117.040	1261.870	52.320
1991	1239.618	1111.190	1329.550	70.791
1992	1233.208	1100.000	1412.380	91.150
1993	1571.915	1475.660	1687.170	65.120
1994	1611.746	1548.290	1699.450	50.286
1995	1631.034	1592.670	1710.890	38.679

This foreign exchange rate is freely determined by demand and supply conditions in the FX markets, but the Federal Reserve and the Bank of Italy can intervene in these markets when necessary, selling or buying the Italian Lira against any convertible currency. The Lira participated in the exchange rate mechanism of the European Monetary System from the start of the system in March 1979 until September 1992.

The purchasing power parity (PPP) theory states that at the equilibrium level, the exchange rate between the Italian Lira and the U.S. Dollar should be equal to the ratio of Italy's and the United States' price levels. To calculate PPP, we begin with the base period of 1978-81, in which currencies were "correctly valued" (defined as a time when the current account balances of the three biggest industrial nations - the United States, Germany and Japan - were close to equilibrium). To calculate PPP for future periods, the base-PPP is simply adjusted for inflation differentials, using producer price inflation as a measure of inflation.

Canadian Dollar Exchange Rate

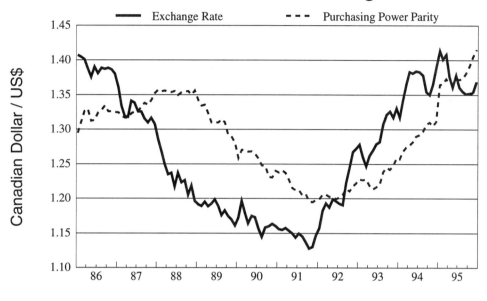

Date Range	Mean	Min.	Max.	Std.Dev.
1986-1995	1.268	1.128	1.413	0.090
1986	1.390	1.376	1.407	0.010
1987	1.326	1.308	1.361	0.015
1988	1.233	1.196	1.286	0.025
1989	1.184	1.161	1.199	0.011
1990	1.167	1.145	1.197	0.013
1991	1.146	1.128	1.157	0.010
1992	1.209	1.157	1.273	0.036
1993	1.290	1.247	1.331	0.029
1994	1.366	1.317	1.389	0.022
1995	1.375	1.351	1.413	0.023

This foreign exchange rate is freely determined by demand and supply conditions in the FX markets, but the Federal Reserve and the Bank of Canada can intervene in these markets when necessary, selling or buying Canadian Dollars against any convertible currency (usually U.S. Dollars).

The purchasing power parity (PPP) theory states that at the equilibrium level, the exchange rate between the Canadian Dollar and the U.S. Dollar should be equal to the ratio of Canada's and the United States' price levels. To calculate PPP, we begin with the base period of 1978-81, in which currencies were "correctly valued" (defined as a time when the current account balances of the three biggest industrial nations - the United States, Germany and Japan - were close to equilibrium). To calculate PPP for future periods, the base-PPP is simply adjusted for inflation differentials, using producer price inflation as a measure of inflation.

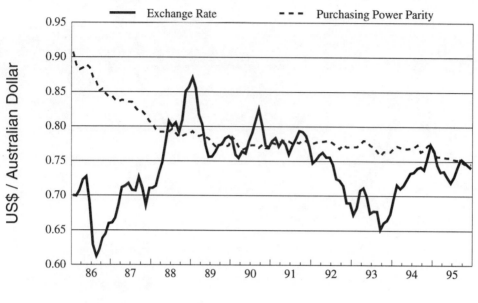

Date Range	Mean	Min.	Max.	Std.Dev.
1986-1995	0.739	0.612	0.871	0.051
1986	0.671	0.612	0.727	0.041
1987	0.701	0.661	0.727	0.021
1988	0.784	0.711	0.857	0.049
1989	0.793	0.756	0.871	0.038
1990	0.781	0.755	0.825	0.022
1991	0.779	0.760	0.794	0.010
1992	0.735	0.690	0.762	0.026
1993	0.680	0.652	0.712	0.018
1994	0.732	0.696	0.774	0.021
1995	0.740	0.720	0.765	0.013

This foreign exchange rate is freely determined by demand and supply conditions in the FX markets, but the Federal Reserve and the Reserve Bank of Australia can intervene in these markets when necessary, selling or buying Australian Dollars against any convertible currency (usually U.S. Dollars).

The purchasing power parity (PPP) theory states that at the equilibrium level, the exchange rate between the Australian Dollar mark and the U.S. Dollar should be equal to the ratio of Australia's and the United States' price levels. To calculate PPP, we begin with the base period of 1978-81, in which currencies were "correctly valued" (defined as a time when the current account balances of the three biggest industrial nations - the United States, Germany and Japan - were close to equilibrium). To calculate PPP for future periods, the base-PPP is simply adjusted for inflation differentials, using producer price inflation as a measure of inflation.

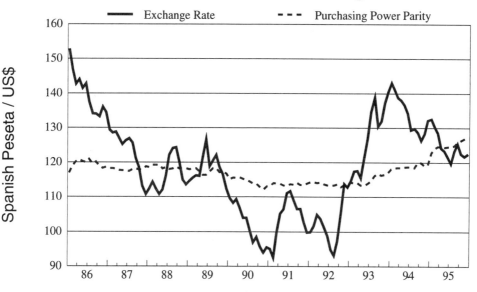

Spanish Peseta Exchange Rate

Date Range	Mean	Min.	Max.	Std.Dev.
1986-1995	119.214	92.530	152.780	13.920
1986	139.989	133.290	152.780	6.115
1987	123.462	110.810	129.410	6.217
1988	116.449	110.820	124.300	4.906
1989	118.333	112.360	126.600	3.897
1990	101.918	93.950	109.650	5.813
1991	103.884	92.530	111.730	6.036
1992	102.309	93.170	113.790	6.346
1993	127.275	114.620	140.520	9.626
1994	133.870	126.350	142.990	5.550
1995	124.646	119.690	132.600	3.902

This foreign exchange rate is freely determined by demand and supply conditions in the FX markets, but the Federal Reserve and the Central Bank of Spain can intervene in these markets when necessary. Spain participated in the exchange rate mechanism of the European Monetary System starting on June 16, 1989; therefore, the Bank of Spain has an obligation to sell or buy Spanish Pesetas against the currencies of the other members of the ERM (Belgium, Denmark, France, Germany, Ireland, Luxembourg, the Netherlands, and Portugal) in order to keep these exchange rates within a pre-established range.

The purchasing power parity (PPP) theory states that at the equilibrium level, the exchange rate between the Spanish Peseta and the U.S. Dollar should be equal to the ratio of Spain's and the United States' price levels. To calculate PPP, we begin with the base period of 1978-81, in which currencies were "correctly valued" (defined as a time when the current account balances of the three biggest industrial nations - the United States, Germany and Japan - were close to equilibrium). To calculate PPP for future periods, the base-PPP is simply adjusted for inflation differentials, using producer price inflation as a measure of inflation.

PART 3
Foreign Exchange Rates

SECTION II
Crosses

Deutsche Mark / Pound Sterling Exchange Rate

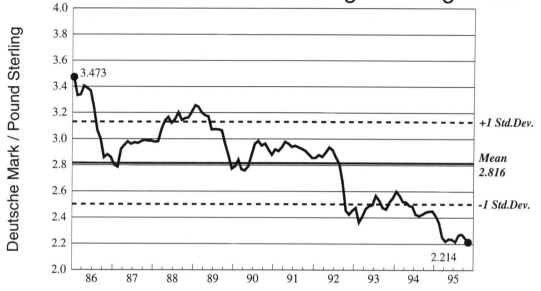

Date Range	Mean	Min.	Max.	Std.Dev.
1986-1995	2.816	2.214	3.473	0.314
1986	3.185	2.861	3.473	0.235
1987	2.941	2.787	2.993	0.072
1988	3.124	2.978	3.207	0.075
1989	3.080	2.774	3.256	0.148
1990	2.875	2.761	2.985	0.082
1991	2.926	2.856	2.979	0.034
1992	2.753	2.424	2.936	0.197
1993	2.483	2.363	2.566	0.057
1994	2.482	2.414	2.600	0.060
1995	2.264	2.214	2.409	0.064

The exchange rate is freely determined by demand and supply conditions in the FX markets, but the Central Bank of Germany (Bundesbank) and/or the Bank of England can intervene in this market when necessary. The United Kingdom participated in the exchange rate mechanism of the European Monetary System between October 1990 and September 1992.

FOREIGN EXCHANGE RATES

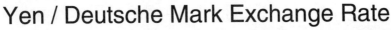

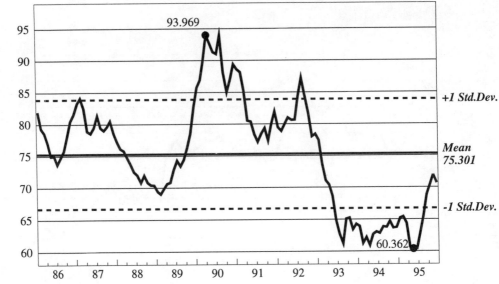

Date Range	Mean	Min.	Max.	Std.Dev.
1986-1995	75.301	60.362	93.969	8.566
1986	77.588	73.714	81.976	2.809
1987	80.429	78.506	84.111	1.926
1988	73.049	70.381	77.215	2.410
1989	73.494	69.030	82.685	4.084
1990	89.580	85.044	93.969	3.072
1991	81.297	77.207	88.596	3.951
1992	81.220	78.035	87.206	2.790
1993	67.340	61.243	77.422	4.897
1994	63.042	60.928	64.704	1.140
1995	65.119	60.362	71.941	4.029

The exchange rate is freely determined by demand and supply conditions in the FX markets, but the Central Bank of Germany (Bundesbank) and/or the Bank of Japan can intervene in this market when necessary. The Yen-Deutsche Mark is the most widely traded cross currency in the world.

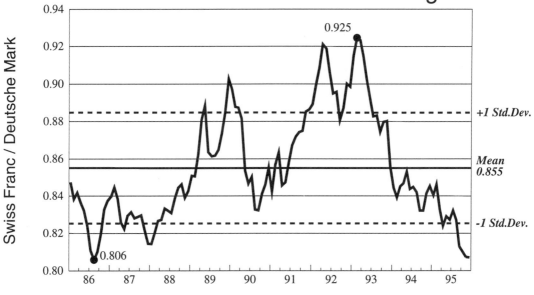

Date Range	Mean	Min.	Max.	Std.Dev.
1986-1995	0.855	0.806	0.925	0.030
1986	0.828	0.806	0.847	0.014
1987	0.830	0.814	0.845	0.008
1988	0.833	0.814	0.846	0.010
1989	0.870	0.851	0.903	0.016
1990	0.859	0.832	0.897	0.023
1991	0.864	0.842	0.886	0.015
1992	0.900	0.881	0.921	0.012
1993	0.894	0.856	0.925	0.022
1994	0.843	0.832	0.853	0.006
1995	0.826	0.807	0.846	0.013

The exchange rate is freely determined by demand and supply conditions in the FX markets, but the Central Bank of Germany (Bundesbank) and/or the Swiss National Bank can intervene in this market when necessary. The Swiss Franc-Deutsche Mark was one of the first cross currency markets to develop.

FOREIGN EXCHANGE RATES

French Franc / Deutsche Mark Exchange Rate

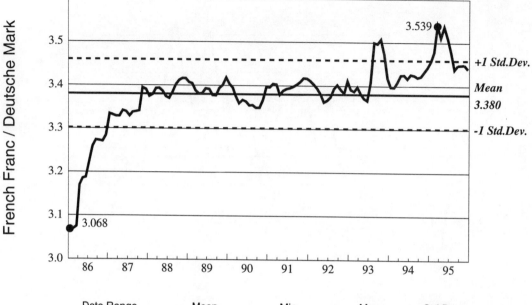

Date Range	Mean	Min.	Max.	Std.Dev.
1986-1995	3.380	3.068	3.539	0.079
1986	3.195	3.068	3.285	0.084
1987	3.345	3.328	3.395	0.023
1988	3.392	3.371	3.416	0.016
1989	3.393	3.377	3.418	0.013
1990	3.369	3.349	3.404	0.019
1991	3.400	3.379	3.418	0.011
1992	3.390	3.362	3.411	0.016
1993	3.425	3.366	3.508	0.054
1994	3.420	3.397	3.443	0.014
1995	3.481	3.439	3.539	0.038

The exchange rate is freely determined by demand and supply conditions in the FX markets, but the Central Bank of Germany (Bundesbank) and/or the Bank of France can intervene in this market when necessary. Germany and France are members of the exchange rate mechanism (ERM) of the European Monetary System; therefore, the Bundesbank and the Bank of France have an obligation to sell or buy Deutsche Marks against French francs in order to keep this exchange rate within the pre-established range.

Italian Lira / Deutsche Mark Exchange Rate

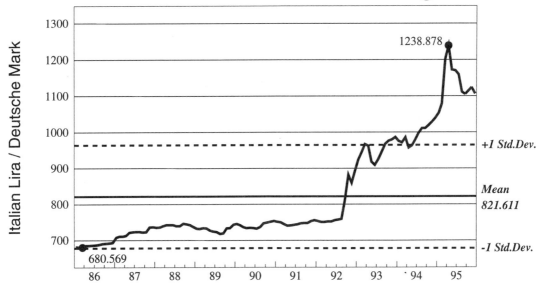

Date Range	Mean	Min.	Max.	Std.Dev.
1986-1995	821.611	680.569	1238.878	143.038
1986	687.238	680.569	693.883	4.446
1987	721.539	708.308	736.909	9.191
1988	741.178	735.853	746.277	3.293
1989	729.926	718.414	743.429	7.197
1990	741.686	732.611	753.744	7.596
1991	747.605	740.923	756.372	4.729
1992	789.971	751.217	892.668	55.947
1993	950.429	909.561	986.361	26.366
1994	994.700	957.413	1039.256	26.777
1995	1138.226	1053.288	1238.878	55.228

The exchange rate is freely determined by demand and supply conditions in the FX markets, but the Central Bank of Germany (Bundesbank) and/or the Bank of Italy can intervene in this market when necessary. The Lira participated in the exchange rate mechanism of the European Monetary System from the start of the system until September 1992.

FOREIGN EXCHANGE RATES

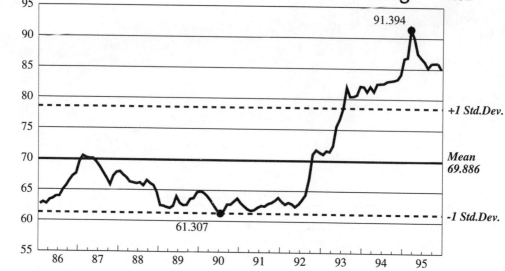

Date Range	Mean	Min.	Max.	Std.Dev.
1986-1995	69.886	61.307	91.394	8.610
1986	64.580	62.656	67.636	1.768
1987	68.662	65.856	70.470	1.521
1988	66.329	64.676	67.969	0.851
1989	62.979	62.085	64.656	0.809
1990	63.063	61.307	64.828	1.137
1991	62.650	61.755	63.871	0.630
1992	65.532	62.441	71.679	3.689
1993	76.900	70.999	82.151	4.382
1994	82.567	81.250	84.078	0.817
1995	87.029	85.017	91.394	1.963

The exchange rate is freely determined by demand and supply conditions in the FX markets, but the Central Bank of Germany (Bundesbank) and/or the Central Bank of Spain can intervene in this market when necessary. Germany and Spain are members of the exchange rate mechanism of the European Monetary System; therefore, the Bundesbank and the Bank of Spain have an obligation to sell or buy Deutsche Marks against Spanish Pesetas in order to keep this exchange rate within the pre-established range.

PART 3
Foreign Exchange Rates

SECTION III
Exotics

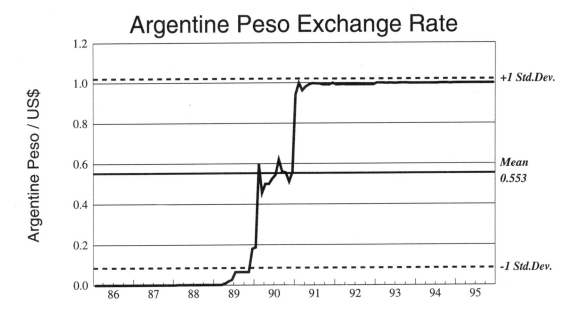

Date Range	Mean	Min.	Max.	Std.Dev.
1986-1995	0.553	0.000	1.000	0.467
1986	0.000	0.000	0.000	0.000
1987	0.000	0.000	0.000	0.000
1988	0.001	0.000	0.001	0.000
1989	0.047	0.001	0.180	0.051
1990	0.510	0.187	0.620	0.111
1991	0.986	0.942	0.999	0.017
1992	0.991	0.991	0.993	0.001
1993	0.999	0.999	1.000	0.000
1994	0.999	0.999	1.000	0.000
1995	1.000	1.000	1.000	0.000

The peso replaced the austral effective January 1, 1992 in a ratio of 1:10,000. All the following data are expressed in pesos. A single tier freely floating exchange rate was adopted in late-1989. This system lasted until April 1991 when the Convertibility Plan was introduced. Under the Plan, the peso was fully convertible into U.S. Dollars at par, and the right to change the exchange rate was ceded to Congress. Since then, the peso has been managed in a narrow band with the (U.S. Dollar) floor set at 1.00. The central bank intervenes regularly to maintain the band, sometimes intervening on both sides of the market during the day.

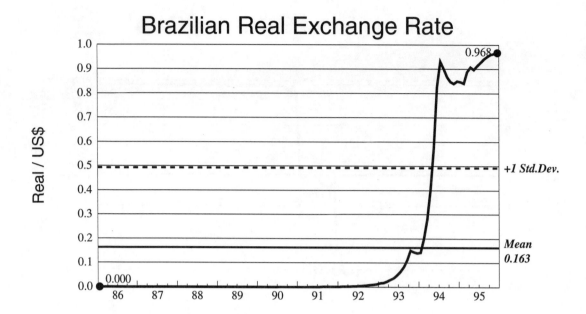

Date Range	Mean	Min.	Max.	Std.Dev.
1986-1995	0.163	0.000	0.968	0.329
1986	0.000	0.000	0.000	0.000
1987	0.000	0.000	0.000	0.000
1988	0.000	0.000	0.000	0.000
1989	0.000	0.000	0.000	0.000
1990	0.000	0.000	0.000	0.000
1991	0.000	0.000	0.001	0.000
1992	0.005	0.001	0.012	0.004
1993	0.072	0.016	0.151	0.052
1994	0.639	0.142	0.930	0.301
1995	0.917	0.841	0.968	0.043

The Brazilian real replaced the cruzeiro real on July 1, 1994 in a ratio of 1:2750. The cruzeiro real itself had only come into existence in August 1993, just one of a long line of currencies used by Brazil during a long period of hyper-inflation. Since the adoption of the real, inflation has fallen to its lowest level in decades, allowing a much more stable exchange rate regime. While the overall trend is still toward a modest depreciation of the currency, on a medium-term basis, the real is now managed within a target zone (current 0.91-0.99 reals per U.S. dollar), which is adjusted periodically. On a short-term basis, the central bank indicates a much narrower trading range for the real, and will intervene regularly to ensure that this range is maintained. The real is not a convertible currency from an external perspective.

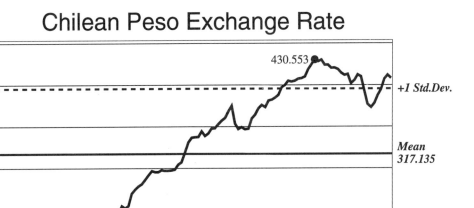

Date Range	Mean	Min.	Max.	Std.Dev.
1986-1995	317.135	185.600	430.553	78.388
1986	194.233	185.600	204.700	6.585
1987	221.158	205.800	238.100	11.039
1988	245.500	240.900	248.900	2.789
1989	269.300	246.000	296.600	17.986
1990	306.417	295.400	336.900	14.632
1991	350.875	337.400	374.900	12.265
1992	362.825	346.800	382.300	13.751
1993	404.472	384.800	425.000	11.371
1994	419.896	401.873	430.553	8.515
1995	396.678	373.264	412.238	14.635

Two exchange rate markets exist: the formal or interbank market and the parallel or informal market. Most transactions are undertaken through the formal market. The rate is determined by supply and demand subject to a band set 10% either side of an official reference rate. The official reference rate is set on a daily basis against a basket (composed of the U.S. Dollar, Deutsche Mark and Japanese Yen) based on the difference between the prior month's domestic inflation rate and the estimated world inflation rate. Following a long period of upward pressure on the peso, the authorities responded recently by revaluing the official reference rate (and thus the band within which the interbank rate trades) by 10%. An increasing number of transactions are being permitted in the parallel market, and the parallel rate trades close to the interbank rate. Chile maintains exchange controls such that from an external perspective the peso is not a convertible currency.

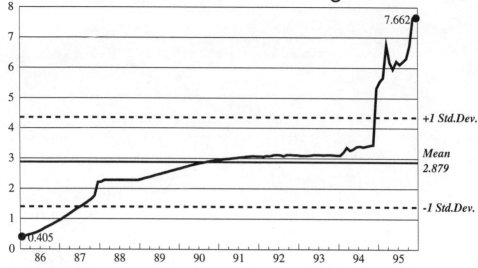

Mexican Nuevo Peso Exchange Rate

Source: Datastream

Date Range	Mean	Min.	Max.	Std.Dev.
1986-1995	2.879	0.405	7.662	1.476
1986	0.634	0.405	0.924	0.173
1987	1.426	0.988	2.210	0.344
1988	2.276	2.221	2.281	0.017
1989	2.475	2.310	2.641	0.110
1990	2.823	2.675	2.945	0.091
1991	3.023	2.959	3.073	0.041
1992	3.099	3.061	3.122	0.023
1993	3.110	3.094	3.123	0.011
1994	3.503	3.106	5.325	0.582
1995	6.419	5.556	7.662	0.675

Since the onset of the debt crisis in 1982, the Mexican authorities have implemented several different exchange rate regimes. The target zone system (know as the "window") was abandoned in December 1994 in the wake of intense speculative pressure on the peso and a massive loss of foreign exchange reserves. At that point, a floating exchange rate regime was adopted, which has been maintained subsequently, despite considerable volatility to the peso. The new peso replaced the peso in a ratio of 1:1000 at the start of 1993, but the name has since reverted to the peso. Mexico does not maintain any formal exchange controls, though some restrictions on local bank accounts persist.

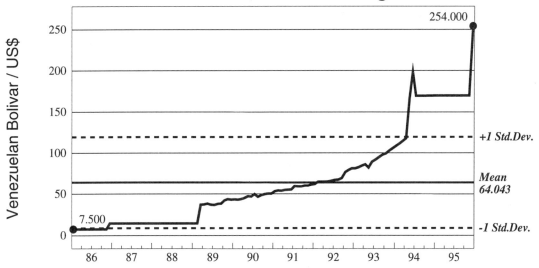

Date Range	Mean	Min.	Max.	Std.Dev.
1986-1995	64.043	7.500	254.000	55.202
1986	8.083	7.500	14.500	2.021
1987	14.500	14.500	14.500	0.000
1988	14.500	14.500	14.500	0.000
1989	35.073	14.500	43.723	9.914
1990	47.014	43.107	50.380	2.787
1991	57.234	53.097	61.554	3.053
1992	69.159	62.007	81.147	6.321
1993	91.441	81.147	105.640	8.537
1994	147.221	108.659	198.330	33.842
1995	177.000	170.000	254.000	24.249

Source: Saladin

Starting in December 1992, the central bank established an informal crawling peg for the bolivar. The system was fine until the second quarter of 1994 when a local banking crisis helped precipitate severe downward pressure on the currency. The government adopted a succession of procedures to moderate pressure on the bolivar, but to no avail. In the end, the exchange rate was frozen at 170 bolivars per U.S. dollar in July 1994, highly restrictive exchange controls were re-imposed along with price controls and interest rate controls. A second-tier market was allowed in the second half of 1995 through the trading of Brady bonds. Growing shortages of foreign exchange, in conjunction with strong inflationary pressures and a rapid depreciation of the second-tier rate, resulted in a devaluation of the official rate to 290 effective December 12, 1995.

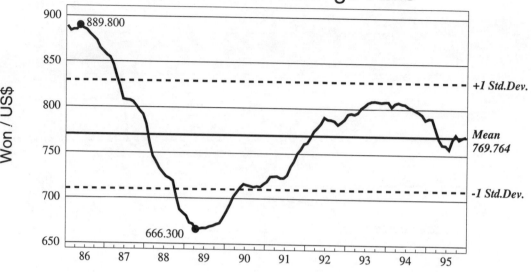

Date Range	Mean	Min.	Max.	Std.Dev.
1986-1995	769.764	666.300	889.800	59.604
1986	880.083	861.400	889.800	9.214
1987	819.683	792.300	857.200	22.990
1988	727.300	684.100	781.600	28.368
1989	671.358	666.300	680.600	4.722
1990	708.583	686.300	716.400	9.638
1991	734.008	719.000	760.800	14.296
1992	781.333	762.000	790.200	8.806
1993	802.608	794.000	808.800	6.254
1994	801.567	788.700	808.100	5.938
1995	771.117	756.924	790.146	10.530

Source: Datastream

Korea maintains extensive exchange controls to the point that the won cannot be considered a convertible currency from an external perspective. The central bank also sets a limit on the intra-day movement of the won/U.S. dollar exchange rate--the current limit is 2.25% relative to the market average rate, which is the weighted average of the previous day's interbank spot transactions.

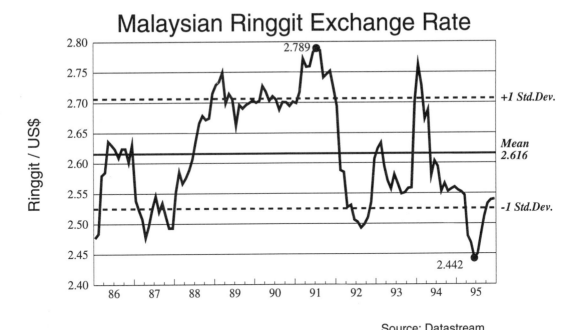

Date Range	Mean	Min.	Max.	Std.Dev.
1986-1995	2.616	2.442	2.789	0.091
1986	2.592	2.477	2.636	0.055
1987	2.514	2.477	2.546	0.021
1988	2.626	2.553	2.715	0.054
1989	2.707	2.662	2.750	0.023
1990	2.704	2.689	2.727	0.010
1991	2.752	2.699	2.789	0.028
1992	2.548	2.493	2.695	0.060
1993	2.587	2.549	2.701	0.045
1994	2.618	2.553	2.762	0.075
1995	2.508	2.442	2.555	0.042

In theory, the Malaysian Ringgit is a freely floating currency, with the rate vis-à-vis other major currencies determined by the interaction of supply and demand. In practice, however, Bank Negara, the Malaysian Central Bank, has periodically taken measures to limit both short-term fluctuations and the role of portfolio capital inflows. This was most evident in the early stages of 1994 when a series of capital and foreign exchange controls were imposed, leading to a pronounced depreciation of the ringgit. Most of these controls have since been lifted.

FOREIGN EXCHANGE RATES

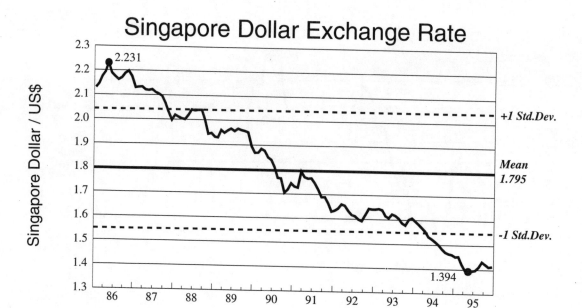

Date Range	Mean	Min.	Max.	Std.Dev.
1986-1995	1.795	1.394	2.231	0.247
1986	2.178	2.129	2.231	0.026
1987	2.097	1.999	2.133	0.043
1988	2.008	1.943	2.041	0.034
1989	1.948	1.894	1.966	0.021
1990	1.808	1.705	1.884	0.065
1991	1.724	1.631	1.793	0.048
1992	1.630	1.592	1.661	0.022
1993	1.614	1.579	1.645	0.021
1994	1.521	1.461	1.596	0.047
1995	1.417	1.394	1.454	0.021

The Singapore Dollar is a freely floating currency, with the rate against other major currencies determined largely by the interaction of supply and demand. The Monetary Authority of Singapore may intervene periodically to prevent unstable market conditions.

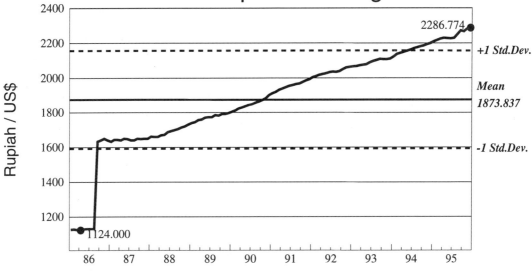

Date Range	Mean	Min.	Max.	Std.Dev.
1986-1995	1873.837	1124.000	2286.774	282.130
1986	1299.333	1124.000	1650.000	252.375
1987	1644.750	1633.000	1650.000	5.396
1988	1689.750	1660.000	1731.000	25.100
1989	1772.083	1740.000	1797.000	18.637
1990	1848.083	1805.000	1901.000	29.122
1991	1954.167	1912.000	1992.000	25.143
1992	2032.583	2004.000	2062.000	18.133
1993	2089.333	2066.000	2110.000	17.270
1994	2164.167	2122.000	2200.000	23.954
1995	2244.124	2210.346	2286.774	26.442

The focus of exchange rate policy is on a gradual depreciation of the rupiah. The central bank sets a reference range of the rupiah/U.S. dollar exchange rate on a daily basis, within which the market rate is allowed to fluctuate depending on supply and demand conditions. The width of the reference range has been increased steadily in recent years, and is currently 44 rupiah wide. Indonesia prides itself on not having any exchange controls, facilitating spot and forward transactions without restriction.

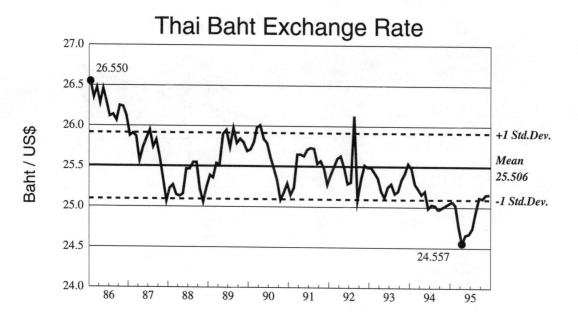

Date Range	Mean	Min.	Max.	Std.Dev.
1986-1995	25.506	24.557	26.550	0.410
1986	26.280	26.070	26.550	0.154
1987	25.698	25.070	25.950	0.260
1988	25.292	25.060	25.550	0.172
1989	25.708	25.360	25.970	0.209
1990	25.594	25.090	26.010	0.312
1991	25.529	25.150	25.730	0.201
1992	25.483	25.090	26.130	0.253
1993	25.318	25.120	25.540	0.134
1994	25.152	24.970	25.480	0.168
1995	24.915	24.557	25.160	0.223

Source: Datastream

The baht is managed against a basket of currencies taking into account the geographic distribution of Thailand's external trade. In practice, this means that the overall pattern of the baht/U.S. Dollar exchange rate closely matches that of other major currencies vis-à-vis the U.S. Dollar, albeit within a much smaller trading range. Trading in the baht is constrained to a range around a daily fixing rate. Most exchange controls have been eliminated during the last few years.

PART 4
Equity Markets

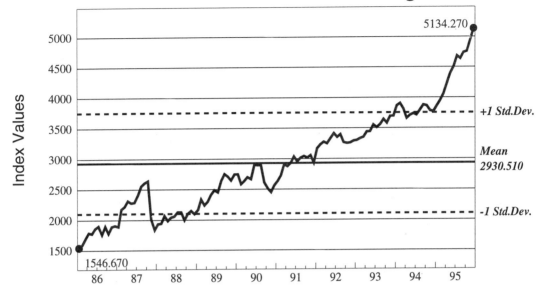

Date Range	Mean	Min.	Max.	Std.Dev.
1986-1995	2930.510	1546.670	5134.270	824.722
1986	1785.223	1546.670	1912.540	121.559
1987	2271.163	1842.340	2639.200	262.162
1988	2055.980	1938.830	2150.960	73.162
1989	2492.788	2168.570	2752.090	204.681
1990	2682.887	2454.950	2900.970	152.712
1991	2929.227	2633.660	3056.350	130.248
1992	3291.963	3168.830	3413.210	70.567
1993	3509.531	3301.110	3697.080	136.253
1994	3793.449	3662.070	3904.700	77.281
1995	4492.884	3870.720	5134.270	398.278

The Dow Jones Industrial Average (DJIA) is the best-known and most often quoted barometer of the stock market, and is the oldest continuous measure of price in the United States. It is currently based on 30 blue-chip issues which represent over one-fourth the value of the stocks listed on the New York Stock Exchange. It is a price-weighted average of 30 large manufacturing companies.

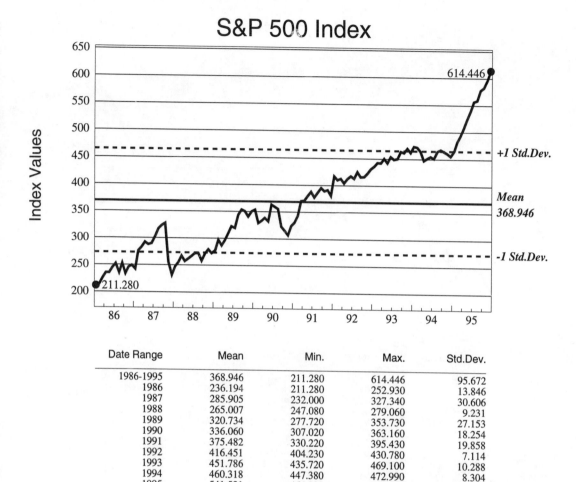

Date Range	Mean	Min.	Max.	Std.Dev.
1986-1995	368.946	211.280	614.446	95.672
1986	236.194	211.280	252.930	13.846
1987	285.905	232.000	327.340	30.606
1988	265.007	247.080	279.060	9.231
1989	320.734	277.720	353.730	27.153
1990	336.060	307.020	363.160	18.254
1991	375.482	330.220	395.430	19.858
1992	416.451	404.230	430.780	7.114
1993	451.786	435.720	469.100	10.288
1994	460.318	447.380	472.990	8.304
1995	541.521	464.980	614.446	47.708

The Standard & Poor's 500 (S&P 500) Index is divided into four main groups which include stocks traded on the New York Stock Exchange (NYSE), the American Stock Exchange (AMEX), and in the Over The Counter (OTC) market. The index includes 400 industrial companies, 40 financial, 40 utility, and 20 transportation companies. The composite index of 500 stocks is capitalization-weighted with the average base level equal to 10 for the 1941-1943 base period. Because of its breadth, the S&P is used as the benchmark against which many money managers compare the performance of their portfolios. The S&P 500 is one of 12 components that make up the U.S. Commerce Department's Index of Leading Economic Indicators.

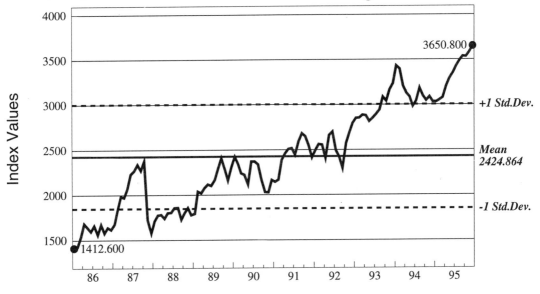

Financial Times Stock Exchange 100 Index

Date Range	Mean	Min.	Max.	Std.Dev.
1986-1995	2424.864	1412.600	3650.800	576.244
1986	1585.308	1412.600	1684.000	89.868
1987	2026.467	1578.500	2373.800	275.197
1988	1792.658	1712.700	1862.200	49.605
1989	2148.408	1793.100	2407.500	164.167
1990	2234.742	2028.000	2422.700	136.199
1991	2458.475	2143.500	2679.600	167.305
1992	2553.183	2298.400	2792.000	140.913
1993	2956.150	2813.100	3233.200	139.706
1994	3142.350	2980.300	3430.700	141.632
1995	3350.900	3030.000	3650.800	218.967

The Financial Times--Stock Exchange 100-Share Index (FT-SE 100) is often referred to as the "Footsie." It was developed jointly by the Financial Times and The International Stock Exchange (ISE) of the United Kingdom and the Republic of Ireland as a counterpart to other market indexes. The FT-SE 100 is an index of the stock prices of the 100 companies listed on the ISE with the largest market capitalization.

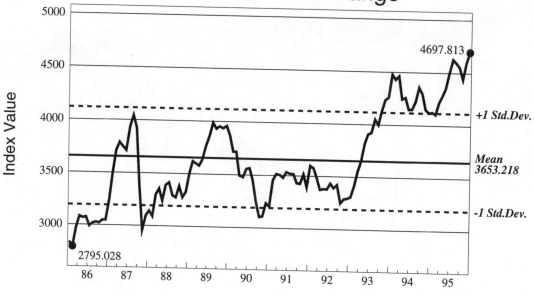

Date Range	Mean	Min.	Max.	Std.Dev.
1986-1995	3653.218	2795.028	4697.813	461.806
1986	2998.156	2795.028	3081.833	91.108
1987	3586.993	2958.490	4044.085	349.944
1988	3288.650	3090.667	3412.874	96.740
1989	3777.522	3511.145	3985.427	178.260
1990	3462.178	3103.718	3867.549	245.378
1991	3458.439	3205.906	3534.202	91.354
1992	3405.741	3249.671	3598.696	107.311
1993	3854.263	3309.089	4258.617	313.126
1994	4276.561	4118.521	4477.507	129.478
1995	4423.672	4104.276	4697.813	205.077

The Toronto Stock Exchange 300 Composite Index is a capitalization-weighted index designed to measure market activity of 300 stocks listed on the TSE, representing 14 industry sectors. The index was developed with a base level of 1000 as of 1975.

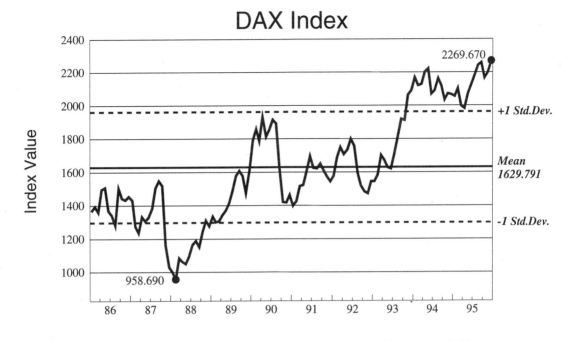

Date Range	Mean	Min.	Max.	Std.Dev.
1986-1995	1629.791	958.690	2269.670	331.938
1986	1412.742	1282.630	1507.320	71.316
1987	1338.915	1030.240	1547.700	152.797
1988	1132.688	958.690	1310.790	109.704
1989	1451.295	1300.520	1612.440	121.334
1990	1731.317	1417.260	1931.300	196.084
1991	1565.917	1398.230	1694.110	88.478
1992	1635.458	1472.570	1798.140	115.877
1993	1771.339	1545.050	2089.780	185.246
1994	2120.718	2034.450	2221.030	58.119
1995	2137.521	1982.220	2269.670	98.145

The Deutscher Aktienindex (DAX) is the newest of the German stock indices and the most widely observed indicator of trends on the German securities market. It was introduced on July 1, 1988 with pro forma information dating back to 1959. The DAX is a narrow-based index of 30 of the most heavily traded blue chip stocks listed on the Frankfurt Stock Exchange (FWB), representing over 75% of the total turnover in German equities. The DAX is a capitalization-weighted total return index with a base level of 1,000 as of December 31, 1987.

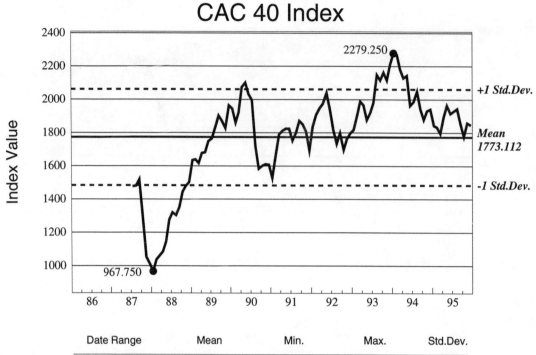

Date Range	Mean	Min.	Max.	Std.Dev.
1986-1995	1773.112	967.750	2279.250	288.965
1986	NA	NA	NA	NA
1987	1305.542	1011.170	1518.600	225.983
1988	1248.047	967.750	1502.090	183.792
1989	1763.383	1618.110	1963.460	115.698
1990	1838.401	1584.900	2100.910	201.112
1991	1768.182	1529.420	1870.820	96.402
1992	1853.986	1697.120	2039.700	105.664
1993	2017.309	1817.250	2212.380	129.137
1994	2058.043	1878.310	2279.250	138.793
1995	1871.327	1778.560	1964.110	58.359

The CAC-40 Index is a narrow-based capitalization-weighted index of 40 of the largest companies listed on the Paris Bourse. The index serves as a basis for futures and options traded on the MATIF and the MONEP, France's financial futures and options markets. The index was developed with a base level of 1,000 as of December 31, 1987, to serve as an underlying index for derivative products.

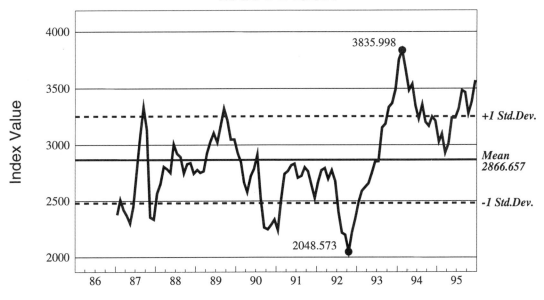

Date Range	Mean	Min.	Max.	Std.Dev.
1986-1995	2866.657	2048.573	3835.998	385.663
1986	NA	NA	NA	NA
1987	2620.833	2302.660	3332.440	364.152
1988	2794.636	2566.180	3006.800	118.270
1989	3014.793	2751.550	3320.860	182.314
1990	2591.403	2247.860	2927.070	257.397
1991	2674.067	2242.670	2832.520	170.195
1992	2484.575	2048.573	2792.697	272.457
1993	2944.967	2487.946	3490.078	344.760
1994	3420.911	3166.023	3835.998	232.386
1995	3253.727	2930.622	3569.633	203.704

The IBEX 35 is a capitalization-weighted index of the 35 largest and most liquid Spanish stocks traded on the continuous markets of the Spanish Sociedad de Bolsas (CATS). The index was developed with a based level of 3,000 as of December 29, 1989, oriented to derivatives trading.

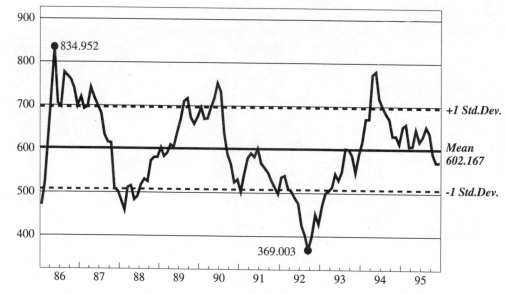

Date Range	Mean	Min.	Max.	Std.Dev.
1986-1995	602.167	369.003	834.952	94.430
1986	694.803	470.231	834.952	106.123
1987	652.363	502.261	741.479	79.898
1988	521.404	459.245	581.818	40.541
1989	644.630	583.802	717.225	45.830
1990	648.862	524.955	751.918	78.437
1991	551.593	498.219	602.445	35.152
1992	461.324	369.003	539.593	56.296
1993	545.224	470.665	602.767	43.153
1994	680.602	615.137	780.632	55.282
1995	620.862	571.525	658.844	31.125

The MIB indices and the COMIT index are the most widely recognized stock exchange price indices in Italy. The MIB indices are based on the prices of all listed shares. The performance indicators comprise a general index and 15 sectoral indices. The MIB Current Index is rebased at the beginning of each calendar year, while the MIB Historical Index's base year is 1975. The MIB Historical Index is shown above.

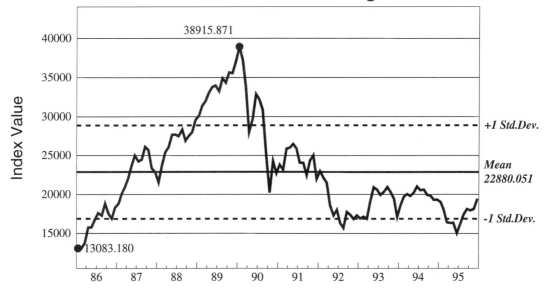

Date Range	Mean	Min.	Max.	Std.Dev.
1986-1995	22880.051	13083.180	38915.871	5995.977
1986	16228.622	13083.180	18820.750	1977.063
1987	23109.012	18820.641	26118.420	2267.982
1988	26672.902	21564.000	29541.461	2193.749
1989	33758.645	30159.000	37132.680	1966.349
1990	29683.047	20221.859	38915.871	5758.327
1991	24446.670	21992.289	26489.000	1458.130
1992	18484.279	15709.450	22983.770	2382.737
1993	19134.666	16879.600	20953.301	1654.788
1994	19908.707	18601.840	21014.730	655.341
1995	17373.955	15039.410	19416.449	1304.542

From its inception in 1949, the Nikkei Stock Average has become the second-most quoted world stock measure after the Dow Jones Industrial Average. The Nikkei Stock Average is composed of the stocks of 225 companies listed in the first section of the Tokyo Stock Exchange (TSE). Most of these stocks are highly liquid and account for approximately 60% of the total market value of the more than 1100 issues listed in the first section. Like the Dow Jones Industrial Average, the Nikkei Stock Average is a price-weighted average. Also like the Dow, the Nikkei's divisor is adjusted either when the composition of the 225 underlying companies is changed, or when any company has exercised its rights for stock splits or gratis issue (ex-rights). The Nikkei Stock Average, when first published on May 16, 1949, had an average price of 176.21 yen with a divisor of 225.

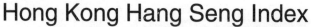

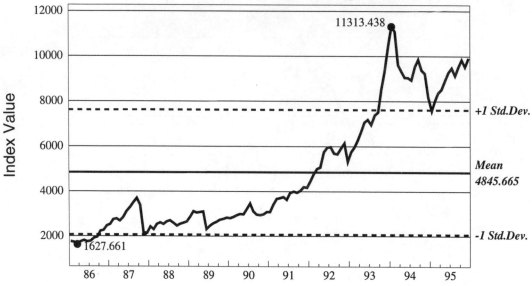

Date Range	Mean	Min.	Max.	Std.Dev.
1986-1995	4845.665	1627.661	11313.438	2772.874
1986	1928.231	1627.661	2468.816	261.187
1987	2910.559	2144.358	3691.870	500.549
1988	2553.112	2312.394	2705.671	109.659
1989	2796.322	2315.358	3114.754	264.067
1990	3031.228	2805.310	3455.940	172.007
1991	3794.724	3082.928	4197.924	322.726
1992	5472.969	4451.041	6137.103	543.047
1993	7419.220	5751.961	10408.146	1385.143
1994	9546.204	8178.466	11313.438	880.820
1995	9004.074	7572.508	9913.412	742.317

The Hang Seng Index is the most widely observed indicator of stock market performance in Hong Kong. It is a capitalization-weighted index of 33 companies that represent approximately 70 percent of the total market capitalization of the Stock Exchange of Hong Kong (SEHK). The components of the index are divided into four subindices: Commerce and Industry (16), Finance (3), Utilities (4), and Properties (10). The index was developed with a base level of 975.45 as of January 13, 1984.

PART 5
Commodities

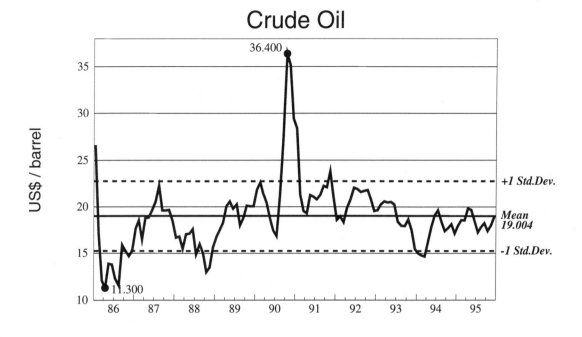

Date Range	Mean	Min.	Max.	Std.Dev.
1986-1995	19.004	11.300	36.400	3.749
1986	14.982	11.300	26.600	4.093
1987	19.175	16.500	22.250	1.434
1988	15.738	13.000	17.600	1.443
1989	19.188	16.800	20.550	1.255
1990	24.083	16.850	36.400	6.571
1991	21.858	19.300	28.400	2.371
1992	20.498	18.350	22.050	1.378
1993	18.963	15.450	20.580	1.605
1994	17.164	14.680	19.640	1.657
1995	18.393	17.260	19.830	0.806

After the oil crises in the 1970's there was a significant increase in the volatility of crude oil prices, that caused an expansion in the consumption of alternative sources of energy. However, crude oil is still the most widely used source of energy. Volume demand for crude oil is most closely tied to economic activity and economic growth in industrial countries. However, from time to time, political considerations also have a great deal of influence in the oil market. Examples of this, as the graph above indicates, were the political events before and after the hostilities in the Persian Gulf from 1990 through early 1991. The largest oil producers are Russia, Saudi Arabia, and the U.S. (which is also the largest consumer). The above data is the nearest contract future price on the New York Mercantile Exchange (NYMEX). Many newly industrializing countries are now significant energy consumers, and so price trends are subject to global economic considerations. Iraq remains excluded from oil exports and the possibility of Iraqi reentry into the marketplace constrains most oil price forecasts.

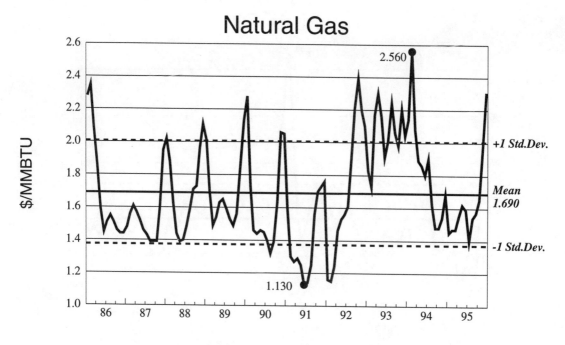

Date Range	Mean	Min.	Max.	Std.Dev.
1986-1995	1.690	1.130	2.560	0.316
1986	1.710	1.440	2.350	0.342
1987	1.529	1.390	1.950	0.156
1988	1.695	1.390	2.110	0.251
1989	1.680	1.490	2.130	0.208
1990	1.639	1.320	2.280	0.320
1991	1.415	1.130	1.760	0.237
1992	1.709	1.150	2.390	0.437
1993	2.053	1.730	2.300	0.172
1994	1.836	1.480	2.560	0.316
1995	1.632	1.400	2.310	0.257

The above series represents spot prices per mmBtu for U.S. Gulf Coast natural gas. Natural gas is abundant, clean, and relatively cheap in North America. Since 6 mmBtu of gas is equivalent in energy to one barrel of oil, and gas is more environmentally friendly than oil, natural gas will consolidate its importance to the economy of North America. Natural gas futures and options markets, as well as OTC derivatives, are now available as price risk management tools.

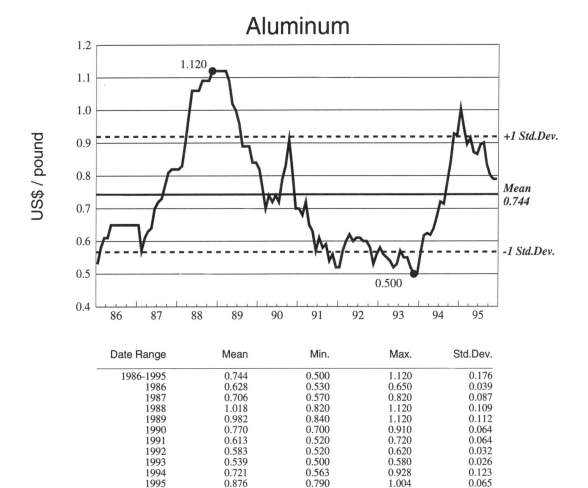

Date Range	Mean	Min.	Max.	Std.Dev.
1986-1995	0.744	0.500	1.120	0.176
1986	0.628	0.530	0.650	0.039
1987	0.706	0.570	0.820	0.087
1988	1.018	0.820	1.120	0.109
1989	0.982	0.840	1.120	0.112
1990	0.770	0.700	0.910	0.064
1991	0.613	0.520	0.720	0.064
1992	0.583	0.520	0.620	0.032
1993	0.539	0.500	0.580	0.026
1994	0.721	0.563	0.928	0.123
1995	0.876	0.790	1.004	0.065

The construction and transportation industries are the largest users of aluminum. The above data is the cash price from the London Metal Exchange (LME).

The surplus in the aluminum market that caused a sharp decline in prices in the early '90s led to a Memorandum of Understanding (MoU) between lead aluminum producers of the world. The ensuing voluntary production cutbacks resulted in aluminum prices doubling over the last couple of years. With the MoU commonly believed to be unraveling, aluminum prices are yet again on the decline. However, an upturn in the global economy could sustain prices at the current level for a few years to come.

Copper

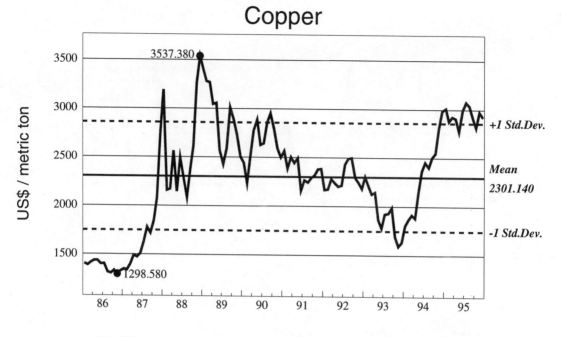

Date Range	Mean	Min.	Max.	Std.Dev.
1986-1995	2301.140	1298.580	3537.380	554.741
1986	1372.441	1298.580	1435.430	51.296
1987	1694.243	1341.120	2729.250	394.152
1988	2572.720	2081.900	3537.380	493.106
1989	2897.712	2426.980	3393.680	329.605
1990	2648.903	2232.680	2949.970	210.756
1991	2368.542	2160.070	2564.970	119.389
1992	2284.208	2168.490	2496.250	120.048
1993	1932.113	1594.770	2302.790	231.586
1994	2305.700	1803.210	2985.020	386.719
1995	2934.813	2773.670	3074.450	88.693

Copper is the world's third most widely used metal. The electrical conductor industry is responsible for 70% of its total consumption. Since 1986 the demand for the metal has increased each year. The U.S. accounts for 22% of worldwide demand. The U.S. is also the leading producer of refined copper. The above data is the cash price from the London Metal Exchange (LME).

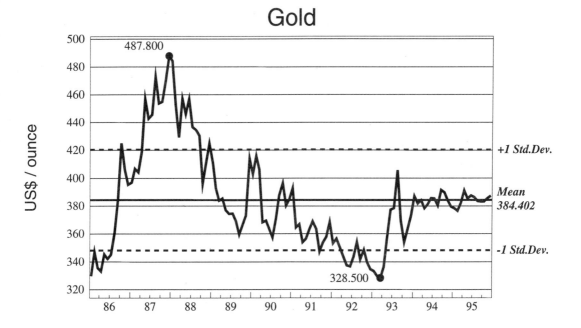

Date Range	Mean	Min.	Max.	Std.Dev.
1986-1995	384.402	328.500	487.800	36.135
1986	362.567	329.700	425.000	32.077
1987	442.525	397.000	487.800	29.479
1988	438.279	396.000	484.000	23.213
1989	381.725	359.400	413.800	16.835
1990	383.629	357.400	415.800	18.606
1991	363.108	347.400	392.750	11.451
1992	345.013	334.600	356.400	7.364
1993	358.867	328.500	405.600	23.725
1994	384.101	378.420	391.430	3.992
1995	384.203	376.570	391.010	3.982

In the financial markets, gold is basically used as a hedge against inflation or political crises by individuals, corporations or governments, and it is the most actively traded precious metal in the market. During recent years the volatility of the gold price has declined substantially due to increased forward sale hedging by gold producers. Gold is also used as raw material for the dentistry industry, for the production of jewelry, and some electrical components. The largest producers are South Africa, the United States, Australia, Russia, and Canada. The above data is the cash price from Handy and Harman.

Silver

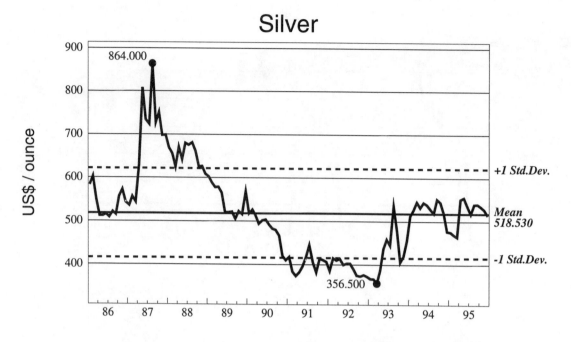

Date Range	Mean	Min.	Max.	Std.Dev.
1986-1995	518.530	356.500	864.000	103.190
1986	541.375	509.000	602.500	32.003
1987	689.208	536.500	864.000	103.976
1988	651.958	609.000	681.000	25.127
1989	549.292	505.500	602.500	34.112
1990	484.125	410.000	526.500	36.464
1991	402.667	373.500	445.000	20.393
1992	393.042	372.500	415.000	16.389
1993	426.250	356.500	535.000	53.124
1994	528.462	477.590	551.980	20.078
1995	518.918	464.580	555.410	31.776

Silver is used as a raw material for several industries, but mainly for the electronic and photographic industries (which account for 50% of the demand). Investors purchase silver to obtain inflation protection, since silver prices respond quickly to changes in the current political and economic environment. 1995 was dominated by movements in warehouse stocks that led to market nervousness and increased volatility over 1994. The largest producers of silver are Peru and Mexico. The above data is the cash price from Handy and Harman.